TALES OF THE KINGDOM

Tales of the Kingdom

Written by David and Karen Mains
Illustrated by Jack Stockman

Chariot Books

David C. Cook Publishing Company, Elgin, Illinois 60120
David C. Cook Publishing Company, Weston, Ontario

Title design and lettering by R.T. II
Chapter title lettering by Robert Propoggio

Library of Congress Cataloging in Publication Data

Mains, David R.
  Tales of the kingdom.

  Summary: Twelve stories centering on the adventures
of two orphaned brothers who escape a polluted city
ruled by an evil enchanter to seek their exiled king
in the place where trees grow.

  [1. Fantasy] I. Mains, Karen Burton. II. Title.
PZ7.M2782Tal   1983   [Fic]   83-5245
ISBN 0-89191-560-5

Classic™ binding, R. R. Donnelley & Sons Company, patents—U.S. pending

To Jeremy
Who has the gift of seeing

TABLE OF CONTENTS

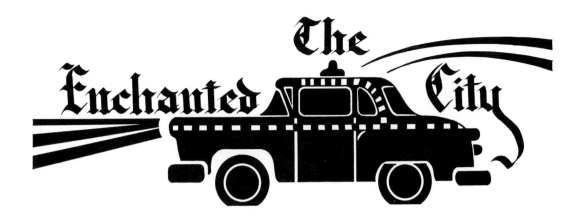

The Enchanted City

Once upon a time, not long ago and not far away, there was a boy, no longer a child and not yet a man, who lived in the Enchanted City. . . .

The boy, Scarboy, and his younger brother, Little Child, were not like the other children in the city. Yesterday, their mother had died, and they had immediately been taken into custody by the Enchanter's men. Rumor said that the Enchanter kept orphans to stoke the huge fires that burned deep in the hold of Dagoda, the temple where the Enchanter lived and ruled.

A Burner, one of the secret police who carried out the Enchanter's bidding, had brought the boys to the Burning Place, a vast square of ashes. There they would watch the funeral ceremonies for their mother, whose body rested on an ornate bier in the middle of the field.

The thought of his mother choked the older boy. She had been so beautiful, as beautiful as the daughter of a king.

"There *is* a King," his mother had always insisted. "A real King." She believed the ancient tales even though signs were posted all over Enchanted City.

THERE IS NO SUCH THING AS A KING.
DEATH TO PRETENDERS.

But his mother had become ill, as so many did in the foul air of Enchanted City. In the last days before she died, she slipped in and out of the fever—often telling Scarboy the ancient tales from her childhood.

"Once a great King ruled our city," she had said. "All the people thought him beautiful and served him willingly. But the Enchanter came and deceived the people and put a spell on the city. The King was exiled. Those who would find him must hunt for him in the place where trees grow—."

Oo-mb-pha . . . oo-mb-pha . . . oo-mb-pha-din—the death drums interrupted the boy's memories. Now he heard the ceremonial bells sewed to the hem of the Fire Priests' robes. He heard the mourners' chants. Then a swish,

9

an explosion! The funeral flames had been ignited.

As the swirling swords of fire leaped toward the sky, a long line of shining cars, low and shadowy and quiet, moved toward the field and parked on the edge of Burning Place. The boy's heart pounded. The Enchanter had come to the funeral ceremony.

Scarboy watched the tall man step out into the field of ashes. The boy saw the amber hair that curled and caught the light of the blazing fire. A handsome man, most thought. But Scarboy's mother had said that the look in his eyes was cruel. The boy took Little Child's hand and held him close.

The Enchanter was wearing the robe of fire, a mastery of woven color: red and yellow patterns interwoven with orange and white and blue. Burners, each holding a glowing poker in their hands, climbed from the other cars. Soon the tall, proud man was surrounded by these guards.

The Enchanter ruled Enchanted City with fire. He loved fire, loved its power. He called it to himself and used it to cast spells. Long ago he had decreed night to be day and day to be night, because he was so jealous of the light of the sun.

Now the people of Enchanted City rose from their beds to work and play and eat when the moon, a lesser light, came up. They went to sleep at dawn. Mothers tucked their children beneath the covers and said, "Morning-morning. See you in the night."

The Enchanter turned and looked across the ash field at the two boys as the drums beat out his personal rhythm, din . . . din . . . din.

"Are these the orphans?" he called, pointing at them.

A Burner nodded.

With quick, long strides, the tall man covered the field between them. Burners marched behind the Enchanter in formation. Each held high a poker, which was now smoldering with hot power. Scarboy covered his cheek with his hand.

The Enchanter faced the boys. The man's eyes widened, then narrowed. Suddenly, the Enchanter reached down and removed Scarboy's hand from his cheek; then the ruler lifted the boy's chin. "What is that on your face? Why were you not outcast from the city?"

The boy squirmed. He wanted to scream for fear. He wanted to kick and run. The man's touch was hot. He struggled to keep calm. "It—it is not a disease, sire. Nor was I born with defect. An accident—an accident at branding."

It was the truth. Long ago, as was the custom when a child was five, Burners had taken all the children of Enchanted City who were his age to brand their hands with a hot poker.

"You are signed with the mark of the Enchanter," the men had cried. "Never forget you belong to the Keep of the Great Burner!"

The boy had screamed, bitten, and kicked. In the struggle, the cruel brand

10

had fallen, either by accident or by purpose, on his cheek. He would bear the scar the rest of his life.

People always looked at him and gasped. They turned their eyes away. Children pointed and shouted, "Scarboy! Hey, you, Scarboy!" Soon he had learned to cover his face with his hand.

Now Scarboy remembered his mother's final words: "Take Little Child and escape . . . escape before branding time, before Little Child turns five. Escape before the Enchanter comes."

But it was too late; the Enchanter held the boy's chin with a vicelike grip. The man bent close and the boy shuddered at the waves of heat. "Your mother foolishly believed in kings," the Enchanter whispered.

How did he know that? Scarboy wondered. He noticed that the Burners' pokers flashed a sudden hot red at the words. The Enchanter's lips smiled kindly, but his eyes were all malice. "And what does her son, her orphan son, believe?"

The boy pulled his chin out of the man's clutch. He covered his cheek again with his hand. He cast his eyes to the ground. "I have never seen a king, sire. Only an enchanter."

The cruel eyes narrowed even more. "Seeing is believing. See that you keep it so, orphan. Keep it so."

With that, the Great Burner turned on his heel, the guard marched beside, and the drums paced: *din . . . din . . . din.*

Then they were gone. Scarboy's lungs screamed for cool air. His heart timed: escape . . . escape . . . escape. He would rather die than be a slave of the Enchanter.

But it was too late for such thoughts. Scarboy felt a strong hand on his elbow. The butt end of an iron poker was shoved into his side by the Burner, whose eyes were hollows of darkness, empty even of the dancing light of reflected flames. "Come," he said. "To the Orphan Keeper with you."

The three moved away from the Burning Place, down little streets, past narrow buildings. Night-lights stood on poles and lit the way. Day was far off. When they came to the market, Scarboy could see the jumble of bins and awnings, could hear haggling and barter. The Burner had released his hold, but it did not matter: his hard poker still jabbed Scarboy's side, and the boy knew he could never outrun his captor. Little Child whimpered and Scarboy lifted him up.

Suddenly, the power failed. "Lights out! Lights out!" people cried.

Power-outs were frequent, but at this precise moment it seemed a miracle. The Enchanted City needed man-made power to live by and to light the night. Everything ran on energy from furnaces beneath the city, which were stoked with fuel. Buses and cars and buildings were attached to underground cables. But the fuel supply was always running low. The man-made power was always failing.

11

In power-outs, traffic stopped. Homes and places of business became dark. The clocks ran off time, on time, in-between time. Even play didn't work. Sometimes the lights failed right in the middle of the ninth inning, just when they were needed most.

But Scarboy knew this power-out was his chance to escape. He bolted away from the Burner, carrying Little Child safely in his arms.

"Runaways! Runaways!" the Burner shouted.

But no one heard him in the confusion. Horns blared! Pushcarts banged against each other! Venders yelled, "Hey! Get that thief! Hands off my stuff!" as vagrants took advantage of the power failure to acquire food. Everyone screamed, "Lights! Lights!" Amid all of this din, Scarboy made a successful getaway.

He ran with his little brother in his arms, ran until his heart felt like bursting.

When the power came back on, Scarboy stopped his frantic running. He had lost his way and he knew that soon the Burners would come looking for them. The Enchanter could not be cheated out of what he owned.

Fortunately, dawn was coming. All would obey the edict SLEEP IN THE LIGHT—except the Burners, who would keep hunting, even though the bright light hurt their eyes. If only Scarboy could stay awake and hide until he found the way out. But what was the way out? Could it be that there was a king, as his mother had said? Would it ever be possible to find the place where this king lived?

Scarboy crept into a hole beneath the porch steps of a nearby house so he could buy time to think. "It's not dark in the place where trees grow," his mother had said. But there were no trees in the city, because all had been chopped for fuel. Scarboy knew trees grew in forests. He had heard there was a forest somewhere outside the city. If only he knew the way.

A timeman walked by crying the hour. Two more hours before day. Suddenly, Scarboy heard the drums. They beat loud and angry. *M-bah-pah-pah-m . . . m-bah-pah-pah-m . . . m-bah-pah-pah-m*. The boy knew they were drumming about him. There was no safety now, no hiding place. Every shadow could hold a Burner.

The boy found a little money in his pocket. He had heard that taxi drivers could get you where you needed to go if anyone could. But would a taxi be safe? Surely taxi drivers knew the message of the drumbeats. Scarboy had to take a chance. He grabbed his brother's hand, carefully looked up and down the street, then hailed a cab.

"Can you get us to the end of the city where the forest is?" he asked the driver as a cab pulled up to the curb.

The driver looked the two boys over with shrewd eyes. "Sure, sure," he said. "But hurry. Curfew's coming. Pay in advance. Refund only in case of power failure."

Scarboy took a deep breath, and the boys climbed in. The taxi driver set his meter and connected the power. Screeching through little-traveled streets, he made his way quickly to a huge garbage dump on the edge of the city. Scarboy had never been there.

"End of the line," the man said urgently. "Passengers out."

Scarboy felt hesitant. "Is this near where the trees grow?"

The driver leaned over the seat and opened the back door. "The line only goes this far. This here's the dump." Then he winked an eye and said, "If you look hard enough, you'll find where the trees grow."

The boys climbed out, and as the cab sped away Scarboy thought he heard the man shout, "To the King!"

To the King! The phrase echoed through Scarboy's mind. But he had little time to wonder about the cab driver's strange farewell, for the familiar sound of the drums—*m-bah-pah-pah-m . . . m-bah-pah-pah-m*—interrupted his thoughts and forced him to look around for a safe hiding place. Or better yet, the beginning of a forest.

Little Child began to cough and whine. "Hush," Scarboy whispered.

The two boys sat on the cinder road. A gray line of light split the sky above the world. Little Child fell asleep, but Scarboy waited for day to come. He listened to the distant drums.

Something is wrong here! Scarboy thought. Suddenly he realized that the shadows were moving! Scarboy was sure he had seen a distant gray form move toward him. That one there! And that one!

The gray in the sky spread. He could see by its light. Over the hills of garbage, men were creeping toward him. *Burners!* thought Scarboy. Without a word, they crept silently closer, one there, another there . . .

The boy bent and lifted his sleeping brother. His knees were weak with fear. He was surrounded on three sides by an advancing menace. He could see them more clearly as the sky began to brighten.

The message drums were sounding far off from within the city, but they were beating faster and faster and faster.

Quickly Scarboy stood erect and faced the shadows. He had not come this far to give up now. He balanced Little Child in one arm and waved the blade of his pocket knife defiantly with the other hand. "No!" he shouted. "I will not be your man! If there is a king, I will find him! If there is a way, I will hunt it out! I will fight you to the last!"

At that moment, day broke behind the boy. The sky flushed pale pink, then warmed to rose. The Burners paused. Their eyes could not bear the bright light.

Scarboy heard a strange and musical humming, which seemed to come from the other side of an old gate he had not noticed on the edge of the garbage dump. The Burners stopped, shielded their eyes, and looked up at the ever-brightening sun.

13

In that minute of advantage, Scarboy turned and ran. He raced with Little Child in his arms toward the old closed gate, away from the Enchanter's stunned henchmen.

Wild weeds grew around the stone gateposts. The wrought-iron latch was rusted. Breathless, the boy stopped and rattled the gate. Just then the sun blazed radiant above them, and the gate began to creak slowly open. Waiting impatiently for entrance, the boy glanced up at the arch. Words were chiseled in the old, moss-covered stones: WELCOME ALL WHO HUNT.

Scarboy squeezed himself and his brother into the ever-widening entrance. He was breathless. Little Child was heavy. How could he close the gate? And where could he hide next?

"You called?" asked a voice behind him.

The boy whirled to face the funniest-looking man he had ever seen. The creature was tall and wore a small tree on his head for a hat. His clothes were a color between green and brown and gray. A giant set of keys dangled from a vine, which circled his waist. He had long white hair and a long white beard and both of them were tucked into his belt. His coat had pockets and his vest had pockets and his pants had pockets—all filled with pruning shears and scissors and trowels.

The man was holding a hatchet, carved with strange markings, in front of his face. Slowly he lifted it with both hands above his head, and Scarboy noticed that the musical hum was coming from the hatchet. The gate slammed shut. The drums outside stopped beating.

All was quiet.

Scarboy was aware of only one sound: *chirp . . . chirp*. What was that? A bird singing? The sound fit his mother's description. But he had never heard its melody before, since there were no wild things in Enchanted City. He looked down at his brother in his arms. Little Child was as quiet as if he were in a deep coma.

"Welcome, hunter," the strange man said and chuckled. He hung the hatchet on his belt. Every move he made sounded with jingling, tools bumping against tools, bumping against still other tools.

"Are you the king?" Scarboy wondered.

"No," said the man, laughing. He walked close and lifted the heavy child from Scarboy's arms. "I am one of the King's men. I am Caretaker. And you are Hero. Welcome to Great Park."

"That is not my name," the boy protested. His empty hand moved by habit to cover his scar.

The man chuckled again. "That is more your name than you know," he said, then turned and walked down the path. Scarboy watched him. Every now and then, Caretaker took a little hop. When he did, every inch of him jingled and chimed. The boy was astonished at this silly creature. *A king's*

14

man, he thought. His wonder increased.

Caretaker stopped and looked back at him. "Come," he called. "We will go to Mercie."

Scarboy watched the man dance down the path. Then he noticed that full day had come. The boy looked around at the trees and bushes and glorious spreads of green grass—all growing things. He took a deep breath and filled his lungs with cool air.

Hero? . . . He would wait and see if such a name were his. *A king's man? . . .* But where, then, was the King? . . . He would keep watch for a king. After all, seeing is believing, as the Enchanter had said.

One thing he did know. His mother had been right: it was not dark in this place where trees grew. There was hardly any darkness at all.

The boy hurried to follow after Caretaker, feeling in his heart as though he had discovered something he had been hunting after all of his life.

And so the boy escaped from the perilous Enchanted City because he was a hunter at heart and hunters always find more than they know.

The Orphan Keeper's Assistant

Once upon a time, the Enchanter decreed that all who had disease or defects that could not be cured would be cast outside the city and left to die. All the unwanted and all the odd were cast out and all those who belonged to no one, except orphans. Orphans were kept because they were useful to the Enchanter.

In the blazing sun, a young woman picked her way across the garbage dump outside the Enchanted City. She wore sunglasses, a wide-brimmed hat to protect her pallid skin, and a large, round button that read: WE LOVE CHILDREN—Orphan Keepers' Association.

She kept slipping on the mounds of garbage. Even behind sunglasses, her eyes were bothered by light. "Whoops! Down again. Watch out! Light's white," she mumbled to herself. "Smats! Huffy-puffy. Garbage dumps are stuffy."

Stained and filthy from her falls, she approached Stonegate Entrance to Great Park. She thought she would rather do anything than go on this wild orphan chase. "Miss a day's sleep. Smudges!" How was she supposed to get these gates opened? She'd never been in this dreadful park before, but this was where the Burners said the orphans had gone.

She rattled the iron gate, noticed a curled potato skin caught on her sleeve, and swept it away. She rattled again. Nothing budged. She tried to crawl over the gate, but her legs kept slipping and her button caught between the thin rails. She finally stood back and hollered, "Does anybody h-e-a-r . . . m-e-e-e-e-e?" Her hat bobbed back and forth. She shifted her bulging basket of a purse and shouted again. "Does anybody h-e-a-r . . . me-e-e-e-e?"

No answer.

She tried another idea. "I am the Orphan Keeper's Assistant! In the name of the Orphan Keeper, open! I am hunting for orphans!"

The gates creaked open. She was impressed by the power of the name she had shouted, never suspecting for a moment that the gates always opened for hunters.

17

Once inside, she followed a path, huffing and puffing all the way. *Whoo! What a jungle. All those trees! Better they were chopped down for fuel. . . . What's all that noise?*

In the distance she noticed a crowd of people in a large field. Some seemed to be dancing. A young man juggled several balls in the air. Then he dropped one. An older man was walking on a tightrope. All were working hard, but they were laughing and seemed to be enjoying themselves. *What a strange place!*

Orphan Keeper's Assistant hurried on, ignoring brightly colored flowers waving on long, green stems and majestic, four-legged creatures, their ears poised to catch any sound. Thankfully, her eyes were shaded by sunglasses; she squinted behind them to keep out the bright light and this dreadful profusion of shape and color.

Orphans were on her mind. *Oh, bother! Orphans and outcasts.* No sane person cared for either. She knew that better than others. Hadn't she been the daughter of an outcast before earning a useful place in the Enchanter's service?

"Nha-a-a, nha-a-a, nha-a-a," the children of Enchanted City had all teased when she was a little girl. "Your mother's an outcast, an outcast, an outcast!"

Her mother had come down with an incurable disease, a malady called heart sickness, and been cast out. Then when her father died, she had become an orphan.

The double chin of the Orphan Keeper's Assistant folded into her neck, and her shoulders shuddered at the memory. She hated outcasts! Nobody wanted an outcast.

The path she followed led to Caretaker's Cottage, all gingerbread trim and fieldstone. A young man, tall and handsome, stepped out the door just as she arrived. He was wearing a long, navy cloak with a silver clasp on the shoulder. She knew from her training that it was the uniform of a Ranger, one of the many watch keepers for the man who called himself the King.

"Can I help you?" the young man asked. His eyes twinkled with light, though his lips were unsmiling.

You certainly can, you nice thing, you, giggled the Orphan Keeper's Assistant inwardly. But she said, "Smats and smudges! Get me out of this light. I'm a perfect puddle in the heat. Is Caretaker home? And what's a mercie? 'See mercie,' the Orphan Keeper said to me. 'Get orphans from mercie.'"

Ranger took her bulging baskets, held the door, and explained, "Mercie is Caretaker's wife. Caretaker is not here today. Step inside. . . . Mercie, someone from the Orphan Association."

The Orphan Keeper's Assistant took off her sunglasses. She saw an old woman standing in front of the fire, older than anyone she had ever known.

18

The elderly lady was stirring the contents of a pot over the fire in the hearth. She wore a long, blue cotton dress, covered by an apron pinafore. Tendrils of white hair curled and fell from beneath a snood. She turned and smiled at the visitor and all the wrinkles on her face creased upward.

"Welcome, hunter," she said. "*I* am Mercie, Caretaker's wife. We are servants of the King." The hand she extended in welcome to her visitor was as smooth and unlined as a girl's and her back was straight.

Odd, the Orphan Keeper's Assistant thought. Mercie seemed both very young and very old. The Orphan Keeper's Assistant felt nervous and confused. *Keep your eye on the odd ones. Be official,* she chided herself. She heard the Orphan Keeper's warning, "Bring 'em back alive. If you fail, you'll have a Burner on your tail."

"I am the Orphan Keeper's Assistant," she announced, loudly, hoping everyone in the room would be impressed. She hooked a thumb under her official button and pushed it out from her blouse. Opening her basket, she produced a signed document. "I have a warrant for errants, here. Signed by Orphan Keeper herself. Two runaways last seen at Stonegate Entrance. One called Scarboy."

Her eyes were beginning to adjust to the dim light inside the cottage, and what she saw astounded her.

Two girls cleared dishes from the extended table, feeling the surface with their hands. Counting with their fingers. They were blind.

Skinny sticks of children ran in and out. *Who would want such skeletons?* Orphan Keeper's Assistant thought. Three children were playing a game on the floor, one with crutches, one not moving. *What kind of hole is this? Who wants outcasts? Yuch!*

Then she spotted two boys who stood in a corner. They moved away from her gaze. The older one hid his cheek behind his hand and held the young one tightly by his other hand. There they were!

The young Ranger made a motion, "Excuse me, Mercie, but I must keep watch. Will you need anything?" he asked, glancing at the woman. But the Caretaker's wife shook her head. With a sweep of his cloak, he was out and gone.

Fool! thought the Orphan Keeper's Assistant. *Do you think this old ditty is a match for me?* She was sorry to see him go. She needed a little romance in her life. An assistant got sick and tired of Orphan Roll Calls, Orphan Head Counts, Orphan Work Shifts, Orphan Manuals. Who needed another Orphan Hunt? The Enchanter's Dagoda was hardly the place for such a sentimental creature as she.

She often dreamed of a nice, young man saying, "Orphan Keeper's Assistant, you are my heart's desire—"

The boy in the corner glared at her. She glared back, then said, "Whoo-ee! It's hot! Hot, I'll say!" She took off her sweater. She plopped in a chair and rolled down her heavy stockings. She wiped her face with a large bandanna she had taken from her basket. She lifted her hat. A rotten tomato fell to the floor. Someone giggled.

You'll get yours! You'll get yours! thought Orphan Keeper's Assistant. But out loud she said, "Whose children are these? They can't all belong to you!"

Mercie smiled again, the wrinkles creasing upward. "They are mine," she said, looking the young woman straight in the eye. "They're all mine. We have no orphans in Great Park. Everyone here belongs to someone else."

Everyone here belongs to someone else? The Orphan Keeper's Assistant had never heard such a silly claim. If she could not prove the two children were orphans, she would have to snatch the runaways and escape quickly.

When Mercie seated herself at one end of the long table in the room, the Orphan Keeper's Assistant made her move. She ran to the boys cringing in the corner, scooped Little Child under one arm and grabbed Scarboy's hand with the other, and dashed for the door.

But, try as she might, Orphan Keeper's Assistant could not drag Scarboy out the door of Caretaker's Cottage. She tugged and pulled. She huffed and puffed. "Smats and smudges!" Finally she gave up and looked quizzically at Mercie.

"We have no orphans in Great Park," Mercie repeated. "These children belong here. You cannot take them unless they leave willingly."

Willingly, eh? A gleam appeared in the eyes of Orphan Keeper's Assistant. "You're old, old," she said to Mercie. "You're too old to stop me."

It was a challenge. The two boys moved quickly back into the far corner.

Orphan Keeper's Assistant settled herself at the opposite end of the table from Mercie. She placed her elbows on the tabletop with her chin in her hands. Mercie took the same pose. The two women's eyes locked.

Everyone in the cottage became still. What was happening? Who would win? Why, oh, why had the strong Ranger gone away? In the corner, Scarboy and Little Child held each other tightly.

The Orphan Keeper's Assistant spoke first. "By the Orphan Keeper. By scars and mars. By pain and sadness. Ills and madness. By Orphan Keeper. Orphan Keeper. You do not belong to Mercie—or anyone else."

Now pains long forgotten by the children in the room were remembered. The boy in the wheelchair hunched and whimpered. The blind sisters bumped into each other. One dropped a dish. One snarled. Another child scratched. The lame child turned his back on his partners.

Mercie looked the Orphan Keeper's Assistant straight in the eye. She answered her spell. "Caretaker! Caretaker! Caretaker's Wife! Whose are these? They are mine. They are mine. Caretaker! Caretaker! Caretaker's Wife!"

Mercie lifted her face from her hands, never taking her eyes from her opponent's face. She threw her arms wide as though she would enclose the whole room. "Things are not what they seem!" she cried. "Things are not what they seem! . . . In Great Park we know this to be true."

The boy in the wheelchair straightened his back. The pain was gone once more. He held his head high. The blind girls helped each other sweep up the broken dish. One whistled a little song. The child with crutches scooted over to his friend. Someone laughed. Two of the skinny children ran out to play.

Orphan Keeper's Assistant was sweating profusely now. Driblets of water ran down her face. Blats! Smats! She'd be fired for sure. Burned by Burners. Where did Mercie's strength come from?

The Orphan Keeper's Assistant made fists of her hands and jammed them down hard on the tabletop. *Ordinary Orphan Hunt. Hah! This is not ordinary at all. Lousy Orphan Keeper. Should have come herself.* She pinned her mind to the boy standing in the corner. *Scarboy, Scarboy, come-come,* she thought. *By the death drums, the Fire Priests, by the fire robe.*

I'll make you come willingly. Over and over she concentrated on Scarboy's name. But the work was hard. Then she noticed the boy take a step out of the corner. She saw him let go of his brother. *Scarboy, Scarboy, come-come.* It would only be minutes before the boy was at her side.

Suddenly the orphan stiffened. *My name is Hero,* he asserted.

Hero? Hero who? Orphan Keeper's Assistant responded to the boy's defiance. *That's not your name. Never! Whoever heard of an orphan named Hero?* Quickly the young woman increased her concentration. She felt the room tilt toward the door. She called in her mind, *Scar-boy, come-come.*

Slowly the boy took another step.

Now! Now was the time! Call out the Names! The young woman rose to her feet, still gripping the edge of the table, her back bent, her eyes pinned to Mercie's. Her voice was shrill. "I am the Orphan Keeper's Assistant! In the name of the Orphan Keeper! In the name of Fire Priests and Burners and Breakers and Naysayers! In the name of the Enchanter! I command all who belong to that burning one to come to me."

The children whimpered. Scarboy began to walk toward the Orphan Keeper's Assistant, his eyes dazed, his steps wooden. He dropped his hand. The raw and ugly scar showed on his face.

Beads of sweat stood out on Mercie's wrinkled forehead. The white hair beneath her snood was damp. But she smiled. She gripped her end of the table. She kept her eyes locked with those of the young woman. She rose from her seat. She commanded.

"I am Mercie, wife to the Caretaker of Great Park. In the name of the Ranger Commander, protector and keeper of the watch. In the power of the Sacred Flames. By the name of the King, Son of the Emperor of All, who will bring the Restoration of the Kingdom. I forbid! I adjure! I prevent."

The house tilted back again. The boy stepped back toward the corner.

Mercie lifted her hands above her head. She clasped them together. "To the King!" she shouted. "To the Kingdom! To the Restoration!"

The children shouted back, their hands clasped above their heads, "To the King! To the Restoration!"

The Orphan Keeper's spell was broken. The children sighed. Mercie slumped. Protection closed over them again.

The Assistant dropped her eyes. A small wail came from her mouth. "Oh, me. Oh, my. . . . 'Find Mercie,' said the Orphan Keeper. I found Mercie. . . . But, Mercie has undone me. I'll get fired. I'll get fired."

The Orphan Keeper's Assistant put her face in her hands and wept. She wailed something pitiful. She blubbered and hollered. She pulled a handkerchief from her basket to wipe her face.

Gently, a tiny hand patted her arm, touched her shoulder, wiped tears away from her cheeks, then her eyes. It was one of the blind girls. The child, smelling of lavender and soap, pressed her cheek against the cheek of the Orphan Keeper's Assistant.

Opening her eyes, the young woman discovered that she was surrounded by the children. The boy in the wheelchair offered a cool cloth, damp and fragrant, to press against her hot forehead. The child on crutches had poured a drink and held it out to her. One of them said, "Don't cry, Orphan Keeper's Assistant, don't cry."

But she cried all the more. Who had ever spoken kindly to her? Her father had died in the Bellowsworks beneath the city and her mother had been an outcast.

Then the two boys standing near the corner came forward. The older spoke to Mercie. "I will go back with her. Little Child can stay with you. Firing is terrible. No one should be fired because of me."

Orphan Keeper's Assistant wailed. She remembered branding. Her hand felt sore at the memory. She was only Orphan Keeper's Assistant because she served Orphan Keeper and the Enchanter without question—not because they cared for her. She had no friends. But Mercie had said, "Everyone here belongs to someone else."

The children patted her hand.

Mercie cleared her throat. "I think I have a happy ending. Why doesn't the Orphan Keeper's Assistant stay? That way, Hero won't have to go back, and she won't have to be fired."

The children danced and jumped. "Yes, stay! Stay, Orphan Keeper's Assistant. Stay with us! Please! Please! We want you to stay!"

The Orphan Keeper's Assistant blew her nose. She sniffled and snuffled. She looked at Mercie. The young woman's eyes were full of wonder. "You want me?" she asked, amazed.

"I have a confession to make," said Mercie. "It was I who called you from the Orphan Keeper. I willed you across the garbage dump to Stonegate

Entrance. I wanted you here. I think you will be very good with the children."

"Stay!" said the blind girl, pleading. "We don't want you to be fired. Live with us! You'll love the King!"

"You can live with us! Hurrah!" cried the lame child. He waved his crutch in the air, tottering off balance, and almost fell. But the Orphan Keeper's Assistant reached out and caught him.

"But why?—" stammered the young woman. "Why?"

Mercie picked up the spoon to stir the pot on the fire. "One more person to love, I guess. Just one more person to love."

Orphan Keeper's Assistant blew her nose. She wiped her face with the damp cloth. "Old woman," she said. "You're no old woman, and that's the truth!"

Mercie laughed. She walked over to the chair where the young woman sat. She put her arms around her and said, "I told you that things are not what they seem."

And so the hunter stayed because she found the orphan she had been seeking—herself. She discovered that the Kingdom was for outcasts, and one must become an outcast in order to follow the King.

The Apprentice Juggler

There was a juggler in Great Park, the land of the King, who wanted to perform with the Juggling Master's troupe more than anything else in the whole world. But he had something terrible hidden in his heart, a secret he had shared with no one man. . . .

The Apprentice Juggler was sure he would shame the troupe in tonight's performance. He knew he would drop a baton during the pyramid cascade. Then, the Juggling Master would know his secret, and he would lose his place in the juggling group. A knot in the pit of his stomach felt like a tug-of-war between giants.

Standing in the middle of the practice field, the Apprentice Juggler warmed his hands in a patch of morning sunlight. He loosened his fingers with limbering exercises. He started tossing balls in a basic crisscross pattern.

The Apprentice Juggler concentrated. He could hear the words of Juggling Master's first lesson. "Teach the balls to dance. The word *ball* is from the French. It means to dance. Make the balls dance!"

The balls did dance in the Apprentice Juggler's hands. As long as he worked alone, he did fine. In this last year as an apprentice, he had learned to toss rings, batons, clubs, and eggs (unboiled ones even). He could spin plates on sticks. He could balance umbrellas on his forehead and shoulders and hands—all at the same time.

He put three balls in motion. *Throw ★ Throwcatch ★ Catch; Throw ★ Throwcatch ★ Catch.*

No one knew he was battling his inner count. No one knew that a different rhythm was ticking in his heart than in his hands.

It was only when the Apprentice Juggler worked with the other student jugglers, or when he did a routine with the troupe, that things went wrong.

He tripped.

He dropped batons.

The others thought this was because he was new at juggling. But the young man knew his inner count was just plain different. He didn't want anyone to know his secret, particularly the Juggling Master. To work with the troupe was the glorious goal of every apprentice.

The balls danced in the Apprentice Juggler's hands. He switched to the two-in-one-hand. He practiced showers. He picked up two clubs. He tested their weight in each hand. He tossed one—high. It turned twice in the air—a double. He started a third club with an outside foot kick up. It turned twice in the air. Soon, even the clubs were dancing.

He guarded himself against his inner rhythm.

One of the other fellows was juggling clubs. He moved closer to the Apprentice Juggler and started passing. Six clubs now looped into the air. The young men timed out loud. "Pass, Self, Self. Pass, Self, Self. Pass, Self, Self, Pass."

So far, so good, thought the Apprentice Juggler. If only he could count out loud as he was now. But every juggler knew that was the sign of an amateur.

"Very good! Very good!" shouted the Juggling Master. "Excellent work this morning! And I have wonderful news. The King will be present at tonight's Great Celebration. We will be performing for him!"

The whole troupe cheered, but the Apprentice Juggler's heart fell to the pit of his stomach, where the tug-of-war was raging. He had juggled at Great Celebrations before, with the other students. Tonight he was supposed to solo, then appear with the troupe in the finale.

What if he failed before the King? It would serve him right for keeping this hidden thing to himself. All he had ever dreamed of was seeing the King smile in pleasure at his juggling. He had even imagined the King walking over to him and saying, "Well, done, young man. You have a special gift."

The Juggling Master's voice interrupted his thoughts. "Let's practice the finale!"

The troupe moved into position for the pyramid cascade. Four jugglers stood in a row. A signal was shouted, "Hup!" All counted inwardly, *One, two, UP!* Three jugglers hopped on the shoulders of the first four.

The signal again, "Hup!" *One, two, three, UP!* A hand grasp, a scramble, a hop. The two apprentices climbed to the very peak.

The clubs began looping upwards, turning and spinning up the pyramid. Eight came from the bottom. Six passed from the middle. The apprentices turned the rising clubs back down toward the outside men. It was quick work, but simple—as long as the count was kept.

The Apprentice Juggler knew that all nine members of the troupe were timing inwardly: *Throw ★ Throwcatch ★ Catch; Throw ★ Throwcatch ★ Catch.*

With horror, he realized his count was off again. He had been silently timing: *Throw ★ Throwcatch ★ Throw!* He caught himself, and

changed his pace—but it was a loud danger signal.

Should he tell the Juggling Master? But how could he bear to have his place taken from him and given to another? What would happen if he followed his inner count? What disaster would befall him?

With sagging shoulders, the Apprentice Juggler walked home from the practice field. Later, with lagging feet, he made his way to the huge clearing in Deepest Forest. Here the Great Celebration always took place, surrounded by the circle of Sacred Flames.

The subjects of the King were beginning to gather in Inmost Circle. The Sacred Flames had been lit, and they flickered and danced in a huge ring. Rangers in their dark blue cloaks stood posted around the flames. The music of celebration had begun.

The Apprentice Juggler watched as celebrants walked through the gateway of flame into Inmost Circle: "making entrance," the ceremony was called. He saw each one become real as he or she did so, for the Sacred Flames showed persons not as they seemed, but as they truly were. All disguises were gone.

The laughter and the music and the joy within the flames called to the Apprentice Juggler. But he held himself back. How could he make entrance with this hidden thing in his heart? Wouldn't his secret be revealed when he became real?

The funny old Caretaker walked through the flames. His form dimmed for a moment in the bright light. Then he made entrance. He became tall, straight, broad-shouldered, wearing the dark blue cloak and silver clasp of a Ranger. Caretaker was not what he seemed. He had become Ranger Commander, chief protector of the park and intimate adviser to the King himself.

The Apprentice Juggler squirmed. He remembered how Caretaker had found him, as a young child, hungry and abandoned, and had taken him to Mercie, who had loved and nursed him. He remembered how Caretaker and Mercie hated dark and hidden things.

He decided to wait for the Juggling Master and tell him the hidden secret that his inner count was different and dangerous to the troupe. The Apprentice Juggler would ask him to choose another for the finale. It was the only way.

A sob shook his shoulders. Nevermore the feel of the batons or the thrill of tumbling objects. Nevermore the weight of the ball popping into his palm, then popping out. Nevermore the wonderful rhythm of the troupe.

They would give his place to another. What would become of him? Where would he belong? The young man knew he would never make a good baker or gardener or forester. He couldn't stand singing or dancing. He had absolutely no desire to be a Ranger. The only thing he had ever wanted to do was make balls and clubs and rings and batons and eggs—unboiled—dance.

28

In anger, the Apprentice Juggler tossed the balls he held. This time he kept his own count. Sure enough, the balls moved at awkward intervals. The juggling was not smooth. The rising and falling rhythms were hazardous. He had to tell his secret. He would never be like the other jugglers.

A beggar was approaching the circle of fire. The man wore a brown cloak with a hood that covered his face. He carried a staff and limped. "Alms! Alms!" he cried. "Pennies for the poor! The poor!"

The beggar stopped by the boy and asked, "Juggler, are you performing in the Great Celebration?"

The young man shook his head. Suddenly he wanted to stutter out his secret. He wanted to say, "I have something hidden in my heart."

The beggar motioned for him to step closer and whispered, "I saw you juggling just now. Keep your own count. Listen to the rhythm of your own timing."

The Apprentice Juggler was amazed. How could a beggar know his count was wrong when he had guarded the truth from everyone?

The beggar laughed. He said, "I understand. My rhythm is different, too." With that, the beggar turned to make entrance.

The boy heard the Rangers shout, "To the King! To the Restoration!" The form of the man was dimmed in the flames, then he stepped into Inmost Circle. A cry of recognition went up. People came running to welcome the new arrival. They shouted greeting and called to one another.

The Apprentice Juggler gasped. He had not been prepared for this becoming. The man stood there, changed. He was as tall as Ranger Commander and handsome. The light from the flames reflected as gold glints in his hair. He bent and swung a little child up to his broad shoulders. Mercie, young and beautiful, now that she had made entrance, ran from a place within the circle and took his hand. She called to her husband, Ranger Commander, who came and saluted the King.

The beggar is the King, thought the Apprentice Juggler. *He had said, "Keep your own count."*

The King raised his one hand, still holding the little child on his shoulder with the other. His voice commanded, "Let the celebration begin!"

Apprentice Juggler raced to make entrance. The jugglers were on first, and he was due to solo early in their performance.

In response to the King's command, the musicians began to play a joyful, foot-tapping melody. It called the subjects out of Deepest Forest, through the Sacred Flames, and into Inmost Circle. The jugglers were gathering at the heart of the celebration. The King and his followers circled 'round them. Everyone clapped in time with the music.

The whole troupe was juggling, each on their own. Some tossed balls. Some looped rings. Then it was time for the Apprentice Juggler's first solo act. All the others stopped.

The young man's heart was in his throat. What if a ball dropped? What if he tripped? What if he couldn't control his count? Then he remembered the Beggar King and his words, "Listen to the rhythm of your own timing."

He listened. A new count was rising in him, his own count. Joy came tumbling. It filled his hands, his heart. The count was different from anything he had ever heard. *Throw ★ Throwcatch ★ Catch ★ Catchcatch ★ Throw; Throw ★ Throwcatch ★ Catch ★ Catchcatch ★ Throw.*

He tossed an orange high, high into the air. Then another and another. He caught the first orange right before it hit the ground. The crowd gasped. He caught and tossed the next falling one off his foot. The people gasped again; then they laughed. The Apprentice Juggler dived for the third, tossed it, turned a somersault, caught the next inches off the ground, popped it back up into the air. The crowd roared.

He heard murmurs. "Oh! He's wonderful!" "I've never seen a juggler like him before!" "How different!"

He went on listening to the inner timing. *Throw ★ Throwcatch ★ Catch ★ Catchcatch ★ Throw.* He juggled and somersaulted and dived and counted. Finally, he was done. The crowd laughed. They clapped. They yelled hurrah and stamped their feet and hands.

The Apprentice Juggler bowed. He stood straight and bowed again. This time when he looked up, he was looking directly into the eyes of the King.

The King was smiling his approval.

"A clown! A clown!" someone was crying. It was the Juggling Master.

"You have the rhythm of a clown!" he crowed. "You look like you can't do it. . . . You look like you might drop something. But you don't! A clown is the best juggler of all!"

The Juggling Master became stern. He shook the juggler's shoulders. "Why didn't you tell me your rhythm was different?"

"Be-be-because," stammered the young man between shakes. "I-I thought I would lose my place in the troupe."

The Juggling Master stopped shaking him. "Lose your place? Find your proper place, rather. Didn't you know that in the Great Celebration, all who desire a place, find a place?"

With that, the Juggling Master put his head back and laughed. "A juggler with the instinct of a clown! Oh, they are rare! They are rare! What a troupe we'll have! We'll bring down the house! We will make the balls *dance!*"

So the Apprentice Juggler lost his place in the troupe, but found another. For all who live by the rhythm of the inner timing, which the King approves, find a place in the Kingdom all their own. More than any, they live happily ever after.

The Faithless Ranger

Long ago, danger always came to the people in Great Park who were the most brave and to the places that were the most beautiful. Men and women were never what they seemed to be, for magic and mystery and wonder were always possible.

But that is not so different from the way things are today.

Not long after the boy, Hero, came to Great Park, he went exploring. He walked down across some craggy hills toward the Duck Pond, past Great Park Gardens and Mercie's Vineyards, then around the shores of Lake Marmo. He skirted the edge of Deepest Forest to faraway Outpost Meadow. Sitting beside Singing Swamp, he opened the lunch of cheese and bread Caretaker's wife had prepared for him. Finally, at midday, he sought the cool shadows of Wildflower Woods.

For the first time in his life, Hero felt content and protected. No Burners chased him. No flames threatened. He did not know who ruled this place, but it was certainly better than Enchanted City.

Suddenly, the sound of laughter surprised him. Following the sound, he discovered a girl sitting upon a stump, with flowers between her bare toes. She was braiding her long, blonde hair. She stopped, arched her arm, and a butterfly alighted on her finger.

She turned at the sound of his coming. At her look, Hero covered his face with his hand. For one moment he had forgotten his terrible scar.

"I woke up late," she said, not surprised to see him. Blowing the butterfly aloft, she continued pulling one flower after another from between her toes, weaving them into the braid. "Welcome to the Kingdom," she said with a smile.

"The Kingdom?" Hero echoed. Everyone knew there was no such thing. Then he stopped; of course, the girl must be pretending. He could play along. "Oh, I suppose your father is the King."

"Oh, no," she answered. "The King is my older brother, as he is a brother to all."

Hero tried not to show his doubts. "Then you must be a princess," he teased, looking at her much-washed pants and shirt.

"Yes." The girl was tying her gym shoes. She stood straight finally, curtsied grandly, pulling out the sides of her jeans with her hands. "I am the Princess Amanda. Welcome, Hero."

Hero choked back a laugh and was surprised she knew his new name. Before he could say anything else, however, the girl spat.

"Can you do that?" she asked.

Anyone can spit, thought Hero. He spat on the ground.

"Oh, but can you do this? Can you hit that toadstool over there?" The toadstool was fifteen feet away and small. Amanda spat again and hit it: bull's-eye! Hero didn't know anyone who could do that. He said so.

"It's a gift," said Amanda. "I have perfect aim."

She spat again and hit a knob on a tree, quite directly. "I was just going to the practice field, but thought I would pick some flowers for my hair. We are practicing for the Great Celebration. What is your gift, Hero?"

The boy thought, but nothing came to his mind. He was pleased when their conversation was interrupted by a cry that echoed through the woods. "How goes the world?"

An answer came back, "The world goes not well."

Then another answer, "The Kingdom comes."

"That's the watch cry," Amanda explained. "It goes from tower to tower. The Rangers keep watch. They guard the park against Burners and Naysayers. They also look for lame things and fire in the forest, and they protect the outcasts. Their hearts are brave and full of courage," said Amanda as she started walking toward the practice field.

"Wait! Wait!" cried Hero. "I don't understand. I don't understand anything."

Amanda stopped. Tendrils of hair were already loosened from her braid. Some of the wild flowers had fallen.

"What is a kingdom? The kingdom of what? Where is the kingdom?"

Amanda's jaw dropped. She laughed in surprise. "Why, that's the first rule of Great Park: A Kingdom Is Anyplace Where the King Rules!"

The boy felt stupid. The answer seemed obvious, but he still didn't understand. "I thought this was a park."

"Of course it is, it's Great Park. And the Kingdom is in it. This is where the King rules in exile. But the Kingdom is not only here. It is anywhere the King is and is obeyed. Someday the King's rule will be restored in Enchanted City—and everywhere. That's why we call out, "To the King! To the Restoration!""

Hero was pondering all this when, suddenly, a loud horn blew in the forest. It was answered by another and another. *Croi-e-e-e-e-e-e-e! Croi-e-e-e-e-e-e-e!*

Amanda dropped the flowers. Her body tensed with action. The smile left her eyes. "Danger!" she cried. "Ranger horns. Sounding warning."

The horns wailed again. Then three short blasts. *Croie! Croie! Croie!*

"Fire! Fire in the forest!" Amanda shouted. "Come! We must help. The horns are calling for help!"

Hero felt a sickening cavern open in the pit of his stomach. Fires? His old fear rose to nauseate him. A vision of smoke and pillars of fire flashed behind his eyes. Death drums and a funeral pyre. The mark on his face began to throb. He covered it again with his hand.

Amanda did not notice. "Come!" she cried. She grabbed the older boy's arm and ran with him in tow through the woods. "We must hurry!"

The two hurried to a large lodge built on the edge of Deepest Forest. Hundreds of Rangers were gathering, men and women wearing long, blue cloaks, with the silver clasp at their shoulders. Some grabbed buckets, some shovels and brooms; then they all rushed into the sprawling building.

Hero and Princess Amanda entered and were pushed along by the crowd to the front of the large hall. On the platform a tall and powerful-looking man was examining maps, barking commands, sending off small groups of Rangers this way and that.

Finally, he turned and motioned for silence. The hall grew suddenly still. The man in the front continued to hold up his hand. Hero noticed that his black hair was streaked with gray. The dark eyes blazed. He looked like he could be a king, if there were a king.

Amanda answered Hero's unasked question. "No, this is not the King. This is Ranger Commander."

"Fire in the forest," announced the Commander. He pointed to the maps spread on the large boards. "Two fires begun at distant points within a short space of time. Here and here."

A low murmur spread through the hall. That could mean only one thing. Someone was deliberately burning the trees and planning to set fire to the entire forest.

"These fires are in the third and fourth forest quad, thirteenth and fifteenth fighting districts. First-alarm response crews are already in positions."

Ranger Commander faced his maps and explained strategy. "Mobilize at once. Spade and hatchet crews on this side and this. Bucket gangs waiting behind. Be ready to set backfires, but wait until the horn blasts signal you to begin. Remember, no more fire than absolutely necessary."

He faced the waiting hall. Hero was awed by the feel of the man's absolute command. "Work hard," he called. "Pray for calm winds. Call on the rain."

Then he shouted, "To the King! To the Restoration!"

The hall reverberated as each Ranger lifted a hatchet and replied, "To the King! To the Restoration!" Then commotion. The tramp of feet. A flurry of pushing as fire fighters raced to their assignments.

In an instant Ranger Commander was standing beside Amanda and Hero. "Come with me," he said to the little girl. "Your gifts of seeing are of value to me. And you, boy, come, too. You can help on a support crew. Amanda will show you what to do when we are finished." The man turned and rushed out of the hall.

Confused, relieved, and strangely disappointed, Hero followed. He wanted both to be a part of the drama and not to be.

The powerful man hurried to a nearby watchtower and vaulted up the outside ladder, two rungs at a time. Amanda and Hero did their best to keep pace.

At the top, Hero looked out over all of Great Park. Was there anywhere else as beautiful? Not in Enchanted City, for sure. The Ranger on duty soon came over to them and pointed to two faint columns of smoke rising out of Deepest Forest.

"Small, early fires," he reported. "Two miles apart. The hand-pump-and-hose team at Lake Marmo can siphon water up to the first position if that fire gets bad. The second is going to be tougher. A backfire ring is probably the best strategy."

Suddenly, Amanda pointed. "Look! Over there to the left." All four squinted. Before Hero could see anything, the duty Ranger pulled a large, curled horn from its place on the watchtower wall. He stepped out onto a narrow balcony circling the structure and blew three short blasts, *Croie! Croie! Croie!*

In a fraction of an instant, the blast was answered from a neighboring watchtower, then the next and the next, then others more distant, and on and on deep into the forest.

"A new fire," Ranger Commander explained to Hero in a grim voice. The man pointed. "See the second swirl of smoke. Now look to the north. The new fire's in the twenty-first district."

Now Ranger Commander turned to Amanda. "What do you see?"

The princess stared out into Deepest Forest. Then, to Hero's surprise, she closed her eyes. A silent moment passed as the girl seemed to lose all awareness of her surroundings. Hero had a feeling she was looking deeply inward at things other people could never see. She answered. "A blue cloak . . . a running man . . . a lit torch . . ."

She opened her eyes. They were wide with horror. Ranger Commander glanced at the Ranger; each of them were shocked to learn that the offender wore a Ranger's cloak. "We are more in danger than we know," the Commander said in a voice thick with concern.

That afternoon three more fires flamed in Deepest Forest, six in all. Hero followed after Amanda, carrying barrels of drinking water to the parched fire fighters who battled ring after ring. The first two flaming areas were

quickly quelled: one doused by water pumped from Lake Marmo, the other smothered by pails of dirt dug from the forest floor.

But the third blaze had begun to lick a hungry path through the forest before the Rangers reached it. The fire fighters hacked with their hatchets through roots and sod at a distance from the rapidly traveling flames. Backup crews loosened a ring of dirt with their spades, and then brushed flammable twigs and leaves away with their brooms so the hungry fire would be starved for fuel.

Still, the angry wall of flame came forward, moving closer and closer to Hero, who was mesmerized by this old enemy and could not move or cry out. He could not even throw down the basket of food he was carrying to the workers.

Soon the fire fighters started the backfire, a wall of flame that quickly sprang up to heaven. The rangers were fighting fire with fire, using the backfire to surround the other flames and leave them nothing to feed on.

Hero was caught in between the two. He watched the flames rise higher and higher, grow hotter and hotter. The boy's eyes began to burn and his vision blurred so he could see nothing distinctly, just massive walls of dark red and orange and scarlet. Yet his body remained stiff with horror.

Drifting smoke seared his throat and stifled his breathing. From far away, he thought he heard the familiar sound of death drums: *oo-mb-pha . . . oo-mb-pha . . . oo-mb-pha. . . .*

Then from nowhere, a Ranger was beside him. He threw the boy over his shoulder like a sack of potatoes, grabbed the basket, and raced back to safety. Mute, Hero watched as the backfire leaped and danced, eating all the brush within the ring. The two walls rushed to meet. Finally the oncoming flames embraced and roared and after a long while died because there was nothing else to burn.

Then a hymn went up from the weary men and women, their faces blackened from smoke. "He is the flame that burns the brightest, leaping upward in the heart of man. He is the ring of fire in each soul who warms all into being. The King! Our King is the King of fire and flame!"

The Ranger who had rescued Hero folded the boy in his long, blue cloak, which smelled a little of ashes and smoke. He reached into the basket, broke apart some black bread, and gave half to Hero. "Not used to fire fighting, eh? Tough work. But I think we're done. This one's under control. Caretaker will finish it for us. Feel that rain in the wind. Caretaker's up to his old tricks. Yes, siree. Rain's comin'."

Hero wondered what the silly old Caretaker had to do with the weather. But sure enough, he could feel the soft touch of cool air on his cheek. *Splat!* A great drop of rain fell, then another and another, then faster and faster and faster.

Above the forest, high in the watchtowers, the Ranger horns blew short, hurried blasts. *Croie! Croie! Croie!*

Almost as if the horns had caused Amanda to find him, she appeared at Hero's side. Her hair was drenched. Her face was streaked with soot, but she danced. She turned 'round and 'round, her hands lifted to the rain. "Oh, that wonderful, old, silly old Caretaker. He did it again. He called out the rain." She threw her head back and opened her mouth, drinking in the fresh water; then she stopped still, as though she remembered something she had forgotten.

"The horns! The horns! They've called council!" For a second time that day, the young girl grabbed Hero's hand and dragged him after her. "I forgot! I forgot! Ranger Commander needs my seeing!"

The boy and the girl raced toward the lodge, two out of several hundred who were answering the summons. When they entered the lodge, they saw Mercie who had set up a first-aid station in the back of the hall. It was a confusion of poultice pots and torn cloth and cots, but the old woman worked efficiently, soothing the injured.

Once all the Rangers had assembled, dripping and exhausted, Ranger Commander walked to the middle of the platform and motioned for quiet. "Divisions!" he ordered.

Everyone in the hall shuffled into order; scrambled crews found each other. Wounded Rangers limped to join their proper teams. Hero watched from a corner.

"All present?" called Ranger Commander.

Counting began: "Division One, present or accounted for, sir." "Division two, present or accounted for, sir." On and on came the cries. Miraculously, not one Ranger was missing.

Then the Commander, with blazing eyes, called, "Amanda! Stand forth! Mercie, Caretaker's wife! Stand forth!" The princess took two steps forward and the old woman walked from the back, a roll of bandages still in her hand.

"Stand beside!" Ranger Commander ordered, and the two took a place on either side of him.

"What do you see, Princess?" asked the Commander.

Amanda closed her eyes and answered. "Again, a blue cloak, a running man, a lit torch."

"What do you see?" Ranger Commander asked old Mercie.

She nodded her head. "The same."

"A traitor," murmured the powerful man. His tone was low, gruff, but all in the hall heard. "A faithless one."

"Ordeal by passage," ordered the Commander.

Scarcely missing a step, the community of Rangers marched one by one into a bare circle outlined on the floor of the lodge—the viewing center—to stand before these three who looked deep into each heart. Those who were pure bore it without shirking, marching into the center and out again. But those who had a shadow on their souls dreaded the time their turn would come.

About midway through the column of Rangers, Mercie made a motion with her hands. The Ranger who was in the viewing center paused. His hand slipped beneath his cloak. Ranger Commander looked at Mercie, a question in his eyes.

She nodded.

He looked at the Princess.

She nodded as well.

At that the faithless Ranger uttered an anguished cry, "No-o-o-o!" He pulled his hatchet from beneath his cloak. Holding it out in both hands, he turned and turned in a wide circle. "Stay away! Stay!"

When the Ranger had cleared a swath around him, he stopped, raised his hatchet, and aimed to throw it at Ranger Commander.

"Who are you?" asked the Commander, absolutely calm, as though his life was not in mortal danger. "And why has your heart turned faithless?"

"I am a King's man!" shouted the Ranger. "I have taken the King's vow! I am part of the watch of the protectors! You have not judged me rightly. You are mistaken."

Mercie's voice was low and sad and gentle. "No, sir. It is you. We have seen."

"Repent," said Ranger Commander, his voice rough. "Repent and do penance. The Kingdom will open to you again."

"I repent not!" The faithless Ranger held the hatchet above his head. "I grovel not! One move and you'll regret it!" He swung his weapon around in warning.

Undaunted, Princess Amanda swiftly grabbed Caretaker's hatchet from the silver belt that girded Ranger Commander's waist. "Let fly and *you'll* regret it!" she shouted. Hero watched as the bold girl pointed the blade toward the center of the empty circle. Carefully, she sighted aim. She swung her hatchet round and round over her head. A hum started, the mysterious humming Hero had heard when he first entered Great Park.

The girl took one step forward and released the singing weapon. It tumbled end, over end, over end, and latched, neck to neck, around the hatchet in the faithless Ranger's hand. Circling still, it lifted the other hatchet out of the man's grasp and carried it *thrum* into the wall far away.

The room was absolutely still. Hero's heart was in his throat. Spitting at toadstools was one thing, but the girl's prowess in combat was another.

Ranger Commander spoke. "You have loved the power of fire too much. It controls you. For the sake of Great Park, banishment into Enchanted City will be your punishment. There you will find enough fire. . . . Pray that it will not burn your soul."

Footsteps echoed through the room, timed and in order. A band of blue-cloaked Rangers surrounded the man in the middle. One tore off his silver shoulder clasp. One removed the long, blue cloak. Another demanded the silver buckle and belt. Finally, another gathered the garments of the faithless Ranger together and placed them in the hands of Mercie.

The Rangers closed ranks around the traitor, and marched him from the hall. A terrible and heavy silence surrounded the weary men and women in the lodge after the faithless Ranger left. For the first time that day, Hero saw the proud head of Ranger Commander droop with weariness. "Pray," he whispered, "that the faithless ones may again desire to follow the King."

What would happen to the faithless Ranger in Enchanted City? Hero wondered. He had not met the King, but the boy knew at that moment that he would rather be among these people who used the King's name than among any others. If need be, he would give his life to Great Park.

And the boy learned that a kingdom is a place where it is not enough to say the King's name. One must do the King's will in the King's way or lose the Kingdom altogether.

A Girl Named Dirty

Forever and always, the Caretaker of Great Park brought those who were hurt or frightened, sick or broken to his wife, Mercie, because she was wise and whatever she touched was made better. . . .

Except Dirty. Dirty refused to become better. Caretaker had found her outside Stonegate Entrance, rooting around for food after a Burner had beaten her. The child was covered with welts and bruises.

When Caretaker approached the girl, she immediately stood to her feet and shouted, "I'm Dirty! I never wash! I never cry! I'll fight anything that raises a fist to me!" Then she fainted from her wounds and hunger.

Caretaker brought her to Mercie. But all of the old woman's efforts could not help the girl to enjoy life in Great Park. Dirty hated the cottage. She despised the people who lived there. She thought Caretaker with his tree hat and jingling pockets was stupid. She hated Hero's ugly scar.

"I'm not going to live with those creeps," she declared one day as she stomped off to the barnyard to make her home with the pigs.

From that day on, she tromped in the mud and slept in the sheds. She practiced pig grunts. She learned pig calls, "Hoi-soi-soi-soi-hoi!" She watched the sows give birth to litters, and made pets of the piglets. And because the pigs were gentle, she loved them.

But she refused to love people.

Another outcast was living in the cottage, a girl Dirty's age who had a disease that had made her crippled. Dirty hated the Crippled Girl because she was ugly.

"Sui! Sui!" she would say to her pigs. "How can they live with that ugly thing? Why don't they just get rid of her?"

Dirty sat on a big sow and watched when Caretaker carried the Crippled Girl on a pallet into the warm sunshine. She heard that crone of a housewife sing songs. Dirty made pig grunts to drown out the sound.

At first Mercie tried to persuade her to come into the cottage for meals, but she would not. Then Mercie carried nourishing lunches to the dung heap where Dirty liked to sit, and she ate there with the girl. Finally, Dirty refused any food from Mercie's hand.

"I'll eat the pig slop," she said. "If it's good enough for pigs, it's good enough for me."

Finally, the wise woman and her husband decided to leave Dirty alone. The girl would have to learn that what was fine for pigs was not always right for children.

So Dirty lived in the pigpen in back of Caretaker's cottage and never left it—except to creep into Deepest Forest on evenings of the Great Celebration. Dirty loved to watch the dancing and the singing and the feasting and the joyful fellowship. She hid herself so well, none of the subjects of the King knew that Dirty watched them on the nights when the Sacred Circle of Flames was lit.

At first, entrance—when all the subjects became real—seemed stupid to Dirty. She had been irritated to discover that the simpering Amanda was really a princess. She had thought Amanda's airs were all bragging. She was furious when Mercie walked through the Sacred Flames and became the most beautiful of women. She had snorted when silly Caretaker had become Ranger Commander.

What kind of tricks were they trying to pull on her?

No wonder they were happy and kind. It was easy to laugh if you were really a princess. It was easy to be kind if you were really beautiful. It was a snap to be good if you had all that power.

But what if you were just ordinary and never became anything else? Life was not so easy then. Dirty hated the subjects of the King all the more, but for some reason she could not stay away from their Great Celebrations.

One night, Dirty hid in the hollow stump of a felled tree, and watched celebrants making entrance through the Sacred Flames. Looking through the dancing fire, she could see that banquet tables were being spread with glorious foods. She had brought a dried ear of corn from the pig trough and was munching on its hard kernels.

Suddenly, she heard someone crying, "Alms! Alms for the poor!" She peeked her head out of her hole and saw a beggar, all ragged and threadbare.

Too late! The beggar had seen her and was coming her way. She grunted and grunted, hoping to scare him off. He peeked into the black hollow of the stump. "Aren't you coming to the Great Celebration?" the man asked.

Dirty climbed out. She got down on all fours and pushed her nose into the dirt. She snorted. She made a pig call, "Hoi-soi-soi-soi-hoi!"

The beggar was not fooled into thinking that she was a pig. "Come," he said. "Come! Go through the flames with me. Be my guest at the banquet table."

Dirty looked at him. She showed her teeth. She grunted again. She said,

"Sui! Sui! Go with you? You're nothing but an ugly beggar! I'd rather be with the pigs!"

The beggar touched her gently on the shoulder. Dirty drew back, but her arm felt warm where his hand had been.

"Oh, Dirty," he said. "Don't you know? All the subjects of the King are nothing more than ugly beggars."

With that, he moved off. She was astonished that he hadn't hit her with his staff or shouted, "You filth! Who are *you* to call me ugly?"

Dirty watched the beggar make entrance. She heard the Rangers salute. She saw the glad clamor of hello in Inmost Circle. She watched the beggar become real. Through the burning flames, she saw that he was the most beautiful man she had ever seen. He was the King himself.

And he had said to her, come with me. . . .

At that moment, Dirty, unwashed and smelling of the pigpen, began to love the King. Longing filled her heart. She wanted to be as beautiful as he.

The music for celebration struck up. The King disappeared into the happy crowd. Dirty hid back in her hole. From her hiding place, she could see latecomers hurrying to make entrance. Far off, hastening through the forest, she spotted Mercie and Caretaker making their way toward the Sacred Flames.

As they approached, Dirty could see that they were holding the Crippled Girl between their locked arms. They were taking her to the celebration.

Dirty wanted a better view. She scooted out of her hole to see if that ugly creature would become real. She watched as the three made the Kingdom vow. "To the King! To the Restoration!" She watched them pass through the flames.

Hah! thought Dirty. Mercie became beautiful. Caretaker became the Ranger Commander. But the Crippled Girl was still deformed.

Wait! Wait! What were Ranger Commander and Mercie doing now? The people parted as they carried Crippled Girl through the crowd . . . toward the King!

Dirty watched as the King smiled at the Crippled Girl. She saw him bend over and lift her into his arms. She saw him cradle that stupid girl's head against his chest. The beautiful man was holding that ugly thing! He was speaking to her.

No! No! thought Dirty. *He asked me!!*

Then, Dirty gasped. The King leaned over and kissed the girl in his arms. At his kiss, she suddenly became real. Her body straightened. She was lovely and shining.

It could have been me, thought Dirty. *If only I had not been so piggish. If only . . .*

Dirty was filled with rage. "Sui! Sui! You stupids! You stupids!" But she was really angry with herself. The girl crawled off into the night squealing.

Back to her pigs she went, back to the only things she had let herself love.

The next morning, Dirty sat on the dung heap and watched Caretaker carry the Crippled Girl into the warm sunlight.

Hah! she thought. *Sui! Sui! She's still an ugly cripple.*

But wait!—the Crippled Girl was singing. The pig girl crept out through the gate so she could examine the Crippled Girl more closely.

Hearing a sound, the Crippled Girl turned her face to look at the crawling girl. Her face was as beautiful as it had been when the King kissed her! Even Dirty knew that no one could possibly think the girl ugly once you had looked into her face. It shone.

So that's what happens when you are kissed by the King, thought Dirty. She remembered the warm, gentle touch of his hand.

The thought of going back to the pigs was awful now. The thought of mud was terrible. The thought of living in the shed, of eating slop, was horrible. Dirty would have given them all up for one more chance to say, "Yes, I'd love to be your guest. . . ."

But it was too late. She had become more of a pig than ever. He would never love her, never kiss her.

When Dirty discovered she was crying in front of the girl with the shining face, she ran into the forest. It took days for Caretaker to find her. When he did, she had clean hands and a clean face. Her hair and nails had been washed in Lake Marmo. Her clothes had been scrubbed in a nearby stream. But she was still crying.

Caretaker lifted her into his arms with a sound of jingling, and carried her, as he did all wounded things, to Mercie.

Mercie was delighted. "Why, who is this?" she asked.

"I-I'm D-Dirty," the girl answered between sobs.

"But you're all clean," said Mercie, meaning to be kind.

"No, no!" the child sobbed all the more. "I've washed and washed, but I'm still dirty. I'm all pig inside. The King will never love me. It's too late!"

Mercie shook her head knowingly. "We shall see what the King has to say about that."

So Mercie took the pig girl to the next Great Celebration. Rangers stood watch all around the outer rim of the Circle of Flames. Dirty pulled on the cloak of one and asked, "Is the beggar coming tonight?"

When the tall man shook his head, no, her heart sank.

Dirty followed Mercie, who had stepped into the fire. The heat seared the pig girl's heart. She felt as though everything inside of her was being burned. The girl screamed, and Mercie put her arms around her. She whispered, "Don't be afraid. The pain is only for a moment."

"It's no use! It's no use!" Dirty cried. "The King is not coming! He is the one I must see. No one else can make me . . . clean." With that the two passed through, and the girl looked up into the unspeakable beauty of the young Mercie, whose long, black hair now brushed her waist.

Mercie took the girl's hand. "Let me tell you a wonderful secret," she said. "All the people of the Kingdom know it. It is one of the first lessons they must learn. The King does not have to come in order for us to see him. He is always present."

Dirty stopped crying. She looked at Mercie. "I don't understand what you mean."

"Listen," said Mercie. She held her finger to her mouth for silence. "Listen and you will hear him speak. Be still. He has something to say to you."

Dirty wiped her tears. She closed her eyes and listened as hard as she could.

Yes, there was something. She could hear someone speaking. It was the voice of the Beggar King. He was saying, *Come, come with me. Be my special guest at the banquet table.*

Dirty kept her eyes closed. *His special guest . . .* She could feel something pouring over her. It flowed down through her, starting with her head, then behind her eyes, all through the knots and gnarls of her insides. It was warm. It was gentle. It was fluid.

Mercie whispered, "It's kingslove, Dirty. Kingslove."

Dirty could hear the voice again. The King was laughing. Then he stopped. He said, "I'm so glad you'd rather have me than your pigs."

The warm flood had reached her toes. Dirty felt as if she were being held by the King, just like the Crippled Girl. She felt his kiss. Mercie was right: you did not have to see the King to be surrounded by the power of his love.

Dirty heard music. The violinists and the harpists had begun to play. It was time for the dance, which began the celebrations. She had watched it many times from the outside. Now she was in its very middle. All the subjects joined hands in one huge circle.

Dirty wanted to dance. She wanted to sing and shout. She turned to Mercie. "The King *does* love me! I'm clean! I'm clean! The King has made me clean!"

Mercie took her hand and drew her into the circle of dancers within the Sacred Flames. Someone took her other hand. The musicians began the beat. The girl knew the dance would begin slowly, then build, that the circle would turn in perfect order, then move faster and faster and faster.

She knew the dance steps. She had watched them many times. But she didn't know the subjects would all sing her song. From all around the dancing circle it rose:

I'm clean! I'm clean!
The King has made me clean!

45

She's clean! She's clean!
The King has made her clean!

And the circle moved faster and faster and faster. The subjects of the King sang and danced, rejoicing. But no one sang any louder or danced any harder than Dirty, who had become Cleone, the clean one.

So the pig girl left her pigs for the sake of One she loved. And she became the clean one, who had a tender place in her heart for all things ugly because she knew a King who could find something beautiful in every garbage heap.

Hero's Quest

Long ago and today and beyond, there was and is and will be a Caretaker who is forever busy making and tending new ideas. But the ideas he loves best are the ones he plants in the minds of children.

"I will never be brave enough to be a Ranger," said Hero one day as he watched Caretaker creating flowers in the middle of Wildflower Woods. The boy sat with his hand covering his scar. People in Great Park never called him names, but the boy was sure he caught them looking at him. He thought they probably talked about him when he wasn't near.

"A new idea," said Caretaker. "Let's try this one and see how it looks. Ta-doo!" The old man motioned with his hands in front of his face. A bright yellow blossom exploded from the end of a stem.

"Ta-daa . . ." said Caretaker again. The flower changed. This time it had an orange center and its petals were flat and rounded, not spiky.

"No, no, no. Not right. Not right." Caretaker shook his head. "Let me see. . . ." He thought awhile, his chin in his hand.

The old man suddenly looked up, a bright light in his gray eyes. "Aha! I know!" He lifted his arms. "Ta-dee!"

The flower trembled, then its petals turned spiky on the inside with a rim of smooth, cupped petals on the outside.

"Ah-hah!" chortled Caretaker. "Perfect. Perfect. Just right. Absolutely beautiful. Now watch, boy. Watch me!"

The old man stood on his tiptoes. His elbows were bent and held upright; then he began to wave his arms. The knives and shears and trowels in his vest began to jingle and chime. "Ta-dee! Ta-dee! Ta-dee!" More blossoms exploded.

Caretaker waved his arms some more. He pointed. "Ta-dee!" Petals and stem. A flash of yellow. "Ta-dee!" The floor of the woods became carpeted with lush, butter yellow blooms, all delicate orange at their centers.

Caretaker twirled around. "Oh, they're beau-ti-ful!" He sat down. "Beau-ti-ful!" He held his middle and laughed for the joy of creation.

Hero was amazed. He had heard that Ranger Commander and this old Caretaker were the same person. The powers contained by each continually surprised him. One had the power of leadership; the other had power over creation. Hero was learning to love both faces, but in different ways.

Caretaker stopped his ecstatic glee. He wiped his eyes. "What were you saying, boy?"

For a moment, Hero couldn't remember. He kept seeing wildflower explosions in his mind. Then he knew. "I said, 'I'll never be brave enough.'" In his heart of hearts Hero wanted to be a keeper of the watch, one of the Rangers who were always brave and true. The boy looked down. He held his hand tighter over his cheek. "I think," he continued, "that you gave me the wrong name."

"Nonsense," said Caretaker. The old man stood. He tucked his beard into his vine belt, stuffed some tools in his pockets, and picked up his hat—a small apple tree in blossom. He took the boy by the shoulders. His voice was low and kind. "Only a boy with the heart of a hero would defy the Enchanter to find a king. It always takes courage to believe."

But Hero knew he had only sought Great Park because he was afraid: afraid of the Enchanter, afraid of Burning Place, afraid of fire and of being an orphan. Hero pulled his collar up to hide his cheek. His voice implored, "Can't you make me brave? Can't you give me a potion to drink or a magic mushroom to eat? You can do *anything*. Can't you make a boy brave?"

Sobered, Caretaker waved a finger beside his head. "Let me see . . . let me see . . . I know! I know! You need a quest. Yes, yes. That's right, a quest. Heroes always have to have a quest."

"A quest?" asked Hero. He hoped it would have nothing to do with walking over hot coals barefoot or standing in the middle of a circle of flames—

"What shall it be? What shall it be?" The voice of the Caretaker interrupted his thoughts. "Rescue a princess? No, no, no! We only have one princess in Great Park and she doesn't need rescuing."

Hero thought about Amanda and agreed with Caretaker.

"How about walking through the thing you fear the most?"

Hero's heart bobbed in his chest. He could hear the crackling of flames.

"No, no, no," chuckled Caretaker, seeing the horrified look on Hero's face. "All things in their right time. Let me see. . . ."

Hero took a deep sigh of relief. Why didn't they just forget this whole quest idea? Maybe he would just wake up one morning and feel brave.

"I know!" shouted Caretaker. He shook his finger in the air. "You must face your greatest enemy in fair combat!"

Who is my greatest enemy? wondered Hero. *Burners?* Cold sweat began to drip down the middle of his back. Maybe there was something terrible and unseen lurking in the darkest shadows of Deepest Forest.

"Now on your way," said Caretaker. "I have other things to do today. Yes, yes. Face your greatest enemy in fair combat."

Hero was puzzled. What a silly idea. A quest. How would that make him brave? If he found his greatest enemy, he would probably find it to be greater than himself. Then who would defeat whom? Maybe Caretaker was playing games with him. If Hero could find Amanda, she would tell him if this quest was real or only some new game. At this hour Amanda would be at the practice field, preparing for the Great Celebration that evening.

Hero never went to Celebrations. He was afraid of stepping through the Circle of Sacred Flames. It was one of the reasons he knew he could never be a Ranger.

On the way to the practice field, the boy met the Woodcutter, who was felling trees in Wildflower Woods. Shafts of sunlight caught gold tones in his hair as he worked. "Careful!" called the man. "That tree is about to go." There was a slow crack as wood splintered, and then the great oak came tumbling and crashing to the ground. Hero's heart was awed by the mighty power of the fall.

"Say, you look like a strong lad. Can you give me a little help?" the Woodcutter asked.

Hero thought he would like to help. He had a quest to follow, but it could wait. He grabbed one end of the cross saw with one hand; the other stayed glued to his cheek, to hide his ugly scar.

"Uh, lad," said the Woodcutter, "you'll need two hands to do this work, two strong hands. The rhythm goes like this: You pull and ease your grip. I pull and ease my grip. You pull and ease your grip. Got it?"

Hero nodded his head yes. He put both hands on his handle of the long saw. He felt naked, exposed now that his scar was uncovered.

But the Woodcutter just smiled. He didn't seem surprised or dismayed. "That's a lad. Gotta use two strong hands."

The boy and the man worked well together. Hero fell into the rhythm. Pull-ease-*pull*. Pull-ease-*pull*. Pull-ease-*pull*. Hero glanced time and again at the Woodcutter. He saw his muscles stretch against his shirt; he saw the man's grace and skill as he worked the tool against the wood. It was fun doing a man's work. Hero forgot that his ugly face was exposed.

In between cuts, the two rested. "Are you one of the King's men?" Hero asked.

"Sure am," said the man, drawing a file across the saw's teeth to sharpen them. Then he winked, "One of the *best* of the King's men."

When the huge tree had been split into stacks of lumber, the Woodcutter thanked the boy. "You're a good hand. I hope the work didn't keep you from anything important."

"Oh, no," answered Hero as he covered his cheek again with his hand. "I was just going on a quest." He felt foolish and hoped the Woodcutter

49

wouldn't laugh. "I'm supposed to face my greatest enemy in fair combat."

The Woodcutter laughed. He hoisted the heavy saw across his shoulders. "Sounds like one of the Caretaker's ideas." The Woodcutter turned to go, and Hero watched him walk up the path, whistling. Then the man turned and called, "Uh, lad, if you're going questing and you meet your greatest enemy, better use two hands." He nodded toward the one Hero was pressing to his face. Surprised, the boy thrust both hands into his pockets. The man grinned, turned again, and soon was gone.

Hero kept his hands in his pockets as he moved down the path toward the practice field.

In a few moments, he emerged from Woodflower Woods. Hundreds of people were busy perfecting their skills on the practice field. A choir was rehearsing songs. A troupe of dancers was working out intricate steps to a folk dance. Hero could hear the Rhythm Master counting the beat, "One-and-two-and-three-and-." Acrobats were perfecting the timing of their double loops and backflips, over and over and up again. One man was balancing on a tightrope. Musicians were tuning instruments.

Hero could see Amanda, along with other archers, drawing arrows across a large bow and aiming at a far-off target. Most of the time she hit the mark. Hero was again amazed. How could a girl have such perfect aim? He chuckled to himself. Rescue a princess? Amanda would never need rescuing, at least not by him.

The archers stopped to take a break. Hero felt hot from the day and tired from the work in the woods. He noticed that large tables were being dragged beneath the shade of trees. He walked over to help, and suddenly remembered the Woodcutter's farewell, ". . . better use two hands . . ."

Hero felt stupid. He had spent his entire life since branding time holding one hand against his face. How good it had felt to work that saw with two hands. He forced himself to help pull the tables into place with both hands.

He carried trays of cheese and meats, bowls of fruits, great baskets of black, round loaves. *I have spent my entire life off-balance,* he thought, amazed at his discovery. *Both hands are for working. The Woodcutter is right. I will be at a terrible disadvantage if I meet my greatest enemy with one hand pinned to my cheek!*

He turned full face and looked into the eyes of the people around him: the jugglers, the acrobats, the clowns. No one pointed. No one drew back in horror. One big fellow clapped him on the back and roared, "Don't just stand around. There's a powerful thirst fixing itself out here. Pour cider into mugs."

So Hero did. He used one hand to balance the bottom of the heavy stone jug, and the other to tip and pour. Two hands, he thought. Two hands are better than one.

He decided to carry a drink to Amanda. He wove his way through jugglers

50

and dance troops until he reached the other side of the field.

When she saw him coming, Amanda laughed. She ran to him and took the cool drink, which had caused drops of sweat to form on the outside of the mug.

"Oh, thank you, Hero," she gasped after gulping the cider. "You saved my life. I was dying of thirst."

Hero laughed at her words. *Too bad Caretaker didn't tell me to rescue a princess,* Hero thought. *I've just saved the life of one; she said so.*

"Have lunch with us," Amanda suggested. "We will be done in half an hour."

The late morning grew warm, and Hero stretched out on the fragrant grass. His arms felt strong, exercised. He folded them behind his head. *I wonder who my greatest enemy really is?* He felt good enough to take on that enemy today.

What's a scar? he asked himself. *Lots of people have scars.* Then Hero had a new thought. Maybe the scar had *healed* here in Great Park. Maybe it was almost gone. Lots of things could happen. He could even become brave. . . . Then he fell asleep in the brilliant day.

Before Hero became fully awake again, he heard a sound like a playful breeze. It was Amanda laughing. Hero had discovered that you always heard Amanda before you saw her. "Wake up, you lazybones. I'm starving. It's time to eat." She prodded him with her toe. He grabbed her ankle with his hand.

She struggled.

He grabbed it with the other and pulled.

She tripped and fell, rolled over, scrambled to her feet, and raced to the tables with Hero chasing close behind her. With two hands he could even topple the Princess Amanda.

Once they were seated at the table, the princess introduced Hero to the juggler's troupe. They welcomed him gladly. Then all became quiet, and a song was begun. Everyone joined hands and Hero held onto those on either side of him. They sang, "To the King, the Ki-ng. To the Kingdom and the King." Hero thought of the Caretaker singing flowers into being this morning. He thought of the sound of the saw cutting into the wood and the rhythm of the cutting. He felt the strong grip in both of his palms. Two hands, two hands . . .

"Are you coming to the Great Celebration tonight?" asked Amanda. "It's country fair and circus and naming-day party and pageant and feast day all rolled into one. It's where all the subjects become as they really are."

Hero thought about the Circle of Sacred Flames, which were ignited around Inmost Circle where the Great Celebration took place. He knew he would really be brave when he could walk through that fire.

After lunch, the two children climbed Piney Hill just for the fun of it. The

52

lookout loomed over the practice field. At the top, they had a bird's-eye view of Great Park. Hero could see Stonegate Entrance and the sleeping Enchanted City beyond. He could see Caretaker's Cottage and a line of Ranger watchtowers. He and Amanda noticed the six charred circles that scarred Deepest Forest after the fire. Acres of trees were burnt. Ugly stumps pointed monstrous fingers and arms in the air. Hero remembered Burning Place. He covered his face.

"Will you stop that!" shouted the little girl, angrily.

"Stop what?" said Hero, surprised.

"Covering your face with your hand. It makes you look so—idiotic!"

Quickly, Hero took hold of Amanda's shoulders and turned the princess around to face him. "Amanda?" he asked. "What do you see when you see me?" Maybe his scar had gone away. Maybe Great Park and Mercie's cottage and Caretaker had done something wonderful for him. None of the people in the practice field had pointed at him or snickered. His heart beat wild with hope.

The princess looked him straight in the eye. "I see a good-looking boy with an old wound on his cheek."

"Oh," said Hero, disappointed.

"But that's not all I see," the girl continued. "I also see a hero."

He shook his head. He turned his back to her so she could not see his face. His voice was low. "I'm no hero. I was supposed to go on a quest today. I was supposed to face my greatest enemy in fair combat. The day's half over, and I don't even know who my greatest enemy is—"

"Whose idea was this?" asked the low, impudent voice behind him. "Caretaker sent you on this quest, didn't he?"

Hero turned back to look at her. He deliberately stuck both his hands into his pockets. "Is it a game? I'm terrible at games."

Amanda smiled. Her voice was very low. "It's no game. He sent me on a quest, too. Sooner or later, he sends everyone on a quest. And we all begin by facing our greatest enemy."

Hero wanted to cover his scar, but instead, he pushed his hands deeper into his pockets. "Did you face your greatest enemy?"

She nodded her head yes.

"Who was it?"

"The same as it is for everyone." Amanda giggled when she saw his perplexed look. "I can't stay around here all day answering questions. I have to go and get ready for the Great Celebration."

"Well, go then," Hero said gruffly. "What's keeping you?" He struggled against a strong urge to give her a push down the hill.

"I can't go," she answered, in her most commanding voice. "You are standing on my gown!"

Hero knew he would never understand. Was Amanda pretending or

53

trying to fool him? All he could see were her shirt and well-washed blue jeans! But in Great Park one never knew. Things were always more than they seemed. He stood his ground, feeling foolish. "I'll get off your gown when you tell me the name of your greatest enemy."

In one lightning move, Amanda purposely tripped him, and toppled him to the ground. His hands had been stuck, useless in his pants pockets. He fell to his back and the girl stood over him, challenge flashing in her eyes.

"Don't you know? Every person's greatest enemy is himself. It is ourselves we have to face before we can make any other quests."

With that she ran off down the hill.

Flat on his back, Hero again heard the words of the Woodcutter. *Two hands . . . two hands.* It was true; if he used two hands for the rest of his life, he would be forced to face everyone and everything, including himself.

So the boy learned that quests can be a journey inward as well as a journey outward. There is a kingdom within that must first be conquered before one comes brave enough to challenge the world without. This is an idea that all caretakers of the soul know.

The Baker Who Loved Bread

Once upon a time, there was a King who walked astride his world—here, there, and everywhere. He became poor in order to be like the people he loved, and he lived among the outcasts in order to feel their pain.

The baking complex was hidden in the heart of Deepest Forest, close to the clearing where the Great Celebrations were held. It was important to the Chief Baker that the breads from his ovens be served warm and fresh at the banquet tables. He had carefully planned this cluster of stone houses where the bakers lived and the many, outdoor clay ovens—some large, some small, some with roaring fires, some with smoldering charcoal beds. Each oven was designed to bake a different kind of bread to perfection.

This baker had worked hard to become chief. His father had been a baker and his grandfather before that, but he had his own particular genius for making bread. His doughs were lighter and more nourishing than any his ancestors had ever kneaded! There wasn't a dough of any kind—wheat or rye or corn—that didn't become tasty and delicious after his touch.

The Chief Baker particularly loved making special breads for the Great Celebrations. He loved to twist and braid dough. He loved to invent new recipes for sweet breads. He loved muffins and biscuits and brioches and croissants. He loved to hear the "Oooohs!" of the King's subjects when, with a flourish, the banquet procession was begun and his many bakers carried his creations into the feast in great baskets.

"Chief Baker's done it again!" everyone always exclaimed. "No one can make breads that melt in your mouth like these!"

Bread, the Chief Baker knew, gave special strength, so he prepared baskets of round, black loaves to feed those who had spent the morning at the practice field. He admired the Rangers, and enjoyed preparing nourishing squash-and-cheese breads for them to carry on watch.

After that, however, he drew the line. He refused to send baskets of bread to the old Mercie, though she had never requested it from him. *She has a fireplace and recipes of her own,* Chief Baker thought. Besides, it would only

55

encourage her and that crazy husband of hers to keep filling Great Park with weird people. If these outcasts had so much wrong with them, they must have done something to deserve it. They certainly were not worthy of the King's bread.

One day the Chief Baker inspected his new invention, a wooden paddle wheel that kneaded thirty loaves of bread at the same time. *Genius,* he thought.

At that moment, Chief Baker noticed someone walking up the path to the open clearing of the baking complex. It was a woman carrying a baby under her arms. Her clothes were ragged.

Chief Baker looked around for his assistant, but he could see that the boy was in the middle of rolling out flaky pastry. All the other bakers seemed to be busy: grinding flour, measuring ingredients, watching loaves in the oven. *I'll handle this intruder myself,* he thought.

Still he hated interruptions. Good bread was a matter of timing. A moment too soon, a moment too late, and all was lost.

"What do you want?" he asked the woman, gruffly, as he met her on the path.

Her baby whined. Its little head hung limply on its neck. "Please, sir," the woman answered. "Some bread. We lost our way in the forest, my child and I, and we have not eaten for two days."

A likely story, thought Chief Baker. These kind of people were always looking for a handout, the lazy things. "Can't you see I'm getting ready for the Great Celebration? We have hundreds of loaves to bake today. I can't be bothered just now. Go find Mercie. She's always feeding your kind."

The baby whined again, and Chief Baker thought that the woman tried to look even more pathetic than she was. He relented a little and drew a map in the dirt. "This is the way to Caretaker's Cottage," he explained.

No sooner had the beggar woman left than Chief Baker spied something moving in the woods. Someone was hiding behind a bush. A Burner, maybe, trying to steal some of his fire. A thief of some kind, certainly.

Chief Baker pretended to be walking down the path into the woods, but he suddenly veered and grabbed a ragamuffin who had been hiding behind a tree.

"Aha!" he cried. "Just as I suspected. A thief trying to steal some bread!" The boy was so filthy that the man held him up and away at arm's length.

"No, sir! No, sir!" said the boy, kicking and squirming. "I was just smelling the bread. It smelled so good."

"And that's all you're going to do. Smell. Don't you dare come into my baking complex. I won't have people finding baked fleas in their bread. Be off with you! If I catch you around here again, *I'll bake you!*"

Chief Baker kicked the urchin a few times until he started running, then threw some stones after the boy as he hurried down the path.

No sooner was the urchin gone than the warning horn blew out of the depths of the forest. *Croi-e-e-e-e-e-e-e-e! Croi-e-e-e-e-e-e-e-e!* It signaled that danger was abroad. The first blast was answered by another, and then the chilling cry traveled on and on and on as one Ranger responded to another.

Chief Baker heard a scuffle in the middle of the complex. Two bakers were holding a stranger who was struggling to free himself. The Chief Baker grabbed a sturdy baking paddle and leaped into the fray. One look and he could tell the man was up to no good. The Baker hit the man with the bread paddle—once, twice, three times—and finally the stranger crumpled to the ground.

"We caught him trying to steal bread, sir," the other bakers explained.

Steal my bread, thought the Chief Baker. *I'll teach you.* He hit the man again and again to make sure he didn't have any tricks left in him, until the stranger scrambled to his feet and escaped into the forest.

Croi-e-e-e-e-e-e-e-e! The warning signal was sounding louder.

Suddenly, a band of the blue-cloaked men and women stepped out of the forest. Several of them were carrying a man who looked almost lifeless.

"Stand back! Stand back!" commanded a Ranger as the bakers came running to see what had happened.

"Stand back! The King has been wounded! The King has been wounded! Make way! Make way!"

A cry of horror went up in the baking complex. The injured person was the King!

"Chief Baker," one of the Rangers called, "help us care for our King!"

"Here! Here!" he answered, eager to do whatever he could.

The King was carried into the Baker's stone house and laid on his bed. Fires were lit in the fireplace. A watch was posted to make sure that no more harm would come, and a signal was sent through the forest for Mercie. She would know how to help. Birds and creatures, the ground itself, moaned the terrible news. *The King is wounded. . . . The King is wounded. . . . The King . . . the King . . .*

"Who has done this?" asked the Chief Baker. But no one seemed to know, because the King had not spoken a word since they lifted his unconscious body from Deepest Forest.

If I discover who has wounded my King, thought the Chief Baker, *I will gladly beat that enemy with my bread paddle.* He remembered how well he had trounced the stranger who had been trying to steal bread.

Mercie finally arrived. She bent over the lifeless and terribly still form on Chief Baker's bed. Her eyes filled with tears. "Give me your hatchet," she said to the Ranger standing by the King. "Quickly!"

She turned the hatchet in the firelight. The flames flickered on the markings. Finally she found the marks she sought. Then with her eyes closed, she pressed them to her lips and the song came, a slow, quiet song of healing and peace.

The old woman walked to the bed and sat down beside the King. She placed one hand behind the young King's neck and one on the arch of his chest. She bent her forehead to his. There she stayed, through the long afternoon and into the night, with the song of the hatchet humming in the room.

All through that long night, the subjects of the King held him in their heart. Each remembered kingslove. And the forest was quiet. Great Park sat waiting. Even the moon lagged in its course. The people who were in the Chief Baker's bedroom marked the King's clear forehead, his high cheekbones, the warm brown hair with glints of gold falling on the pillows, the pallid skin.

Finally, near morning, Mercie stood to her feet. She looked as pale as the King. "He will be all right," she whispered. "The wound has been overcome. Feed him when he wakes and lead me to another bedroom."

Each person in the room felt weak with relief at Mercie's words. They felt like laughing and crying at the same time. Within seconds, the Ranger cry sped through Deepest Forest. "How goes the world?"

"The world goes not well. . . ."

"But the Kingdom comes! . . . The Kingdom comes!"

All knew, from the littlest to the largest, that the King was now well and the Kingdom intact. They went about their work with glad hearts as the birds greeted the dawn.

Later, Chief Baker carried a tray of his finest breads into the bedroom where the King was resting. He was relieved to find the King sitting jauntily in bed. One leg was arched under the covers and his arms were draped over the back of the bedstead.

"Had a little tussle in the woods, eh, m'Lord?" the Chief Baker said heartily, trying to cover his concern for the King's health. He set down the breakfast tray, and the warm aroma of biscuits and sweet breads filled the room.

"Might say," answered the King, tearing at a warm and fragrant loaf, which was filled with juicy berries. He bowed his head. "For life and that which sustains it," he whispered. He took a bite and continued speaking, "Like I always say, 'If you're going to get bested by trouble, get bested near the baking complex. The Chief Baker will see that you're fed. He'll feed you like a king.'"

Chief Baker blushed with pleasure. Attempting to be modest, he replied, "Well, sire, it's the King's bread."

The King took another bite. He smiled and in a quiet voice said, "Yes. King's bread is for the King's people, isn't it?"

The Baker was bustling around, opening the window, stirring the fire.

58

"Yes, sire," he said. He remembered the King so still and lifeless. He remembered the long night of fear. Suddenly the emotion of all that had happened overwhelmed him. He choked back tears. He looked the King right in the eyes. "You know, my Lord. If I knew who it was that wounded you, I'd fix him, I would."

"Would you?" answered the King, and set down the goblet that was in his hand.

The room became very quiet. The King moved the breakfast tray from his lap, swung out of bed, and walked to the window. Chief Baker watched his broad back, dark against the morning light.

The sound of busy workers reached them. Bakers singing as they mixed dough. Bellows blowing. The slamming of oven doors. People calling to one another. The warm, fragrant smell of good things baking floated into the room.

"You know, Baker," said the King, turning around to look at the Chief Baker, "my wounds are not like those of other men. . . ."

Chief Baker stopped his fussing about. He wondered what the King could mean.

"When even one of my people is hungry, Baker," the King said, "it famishes me. When a little child is beaten, I suffer. If even my enemy feels pain, I hurt."

The Chief Baker was puzzled for a moment. Then, with an awful rush of memory, he saw the face of a fainting woman he had sent away. He saw the eyes of the filthy child he had kicked and stoned. He heard the cry of the stranger as he had struck him again and again with the paddle. He saw the stranger's body crumpled on the ground; the pain in his eyes resembled the look in the eyes of his King.

"Baker, it is you who has wounded me, even you."

The Chief Baker fell to his knees. "Not I, my Lord! Not I!" But he knew it was true. He was haunted by a face and by eyes and by a cry. He had given one dirt, one stones, and the other beatings.

The King turned. The gold in his hair shone. The light was radiant around his head. It fell across the room and cast the King's shadow over the bent form of the Chief Baker.

"My Lord, what can I do? What can I do?" cried Chief Baker, his head now bowed to his knees on the floor.

The King answered, "Feed the hungry."

The King walked over to the man kneeling in horror on the bedroom floor. He lifted him up and embraced him. He whispered, "Feed the hungry. Then I will be full. . . ." He turned and left, striding out the door as though he had never had a brush with death.

From that time on, the Chief Baker made sure that baskets of bread were taken to Outcast Village for any who had no way to make their own.

Knapsacks of emergency rations were stored at each Ranger watchtower to nourish any who were in danger or who had lost their way—whether they were evil or good at heart. Plates of rolls and trays of tarts were always kept on hand in the baking complex to welcome visitors. And gingerbread cookies, shaped like animals and decorated with sugar icing, were tucked into boxes and sent to Mercie's cottage for the children.

And the Baker discovered that one could love the work of one's hands too much, and that one should always love one's King more. Love for the King is measured by one's love for his people. So the Baker fed the hungry and fed them well—lest the One he loved the most should starve.

Sighting Day

The subjects of the Kingdom worked hard keeping Great Park beautiful. Some were gardeners. Some were foresters. Some were vinedressers. Some were experts on animal husbandry. Some were guides for strangers. Some were healers. But no matter how hard they worked, they loved to play. The game the children played best was seek-the-King. . . .

"I saw the King!" exclaimed Amanda as she burst breathlessly into Mercie's cottage. Two little red foxes came bounding through the door after her, one bumping to a halt on top of the other. "I saw the King on Sighting Day!" she repeated, proud of her success.

"How wonderful!" replied Mercie, who had just walked Man-Who-Sat-Like-Stone to a chair by a window where the sun shone in. Once seated, the man didn't move. He didn't turn his head. He didn't say a word. Mercie said he must have experienced some awful grief in his life.

Hero's little brother often crawled into the man's lap and patted his cheek, but still he didn't move. In a way, they were two of a kind. Little Child never said a word and the man never laughed. Often the two sat quietly together in the sunshine.

"Sighting Day means the King takes time to play," Amanda said, turning to explain to Hero, who was still too cautious for the lively girl.

"The children try to find the King all over Great Park on Sighting Day," Mercie explained further. "It is a huge game of seek-the-King. He appears in disguises, and once a child makes a sighting, he can go to the practice field where the King and the children play the rest of the afternoon. Why don't you try to sight the King, Hero?"

Hero shook his head no, so Amanda bounded out the door without him. She laughed as she ran, and the boy watched the foxes gamboling at her heels down the path toward Wildflower Woods.

It was no use. He would never "sight" the King. Every time someone had whispered, "There's the King!" Hero had only seen a beggar or a woodcutter or a gardener. Never a king.

62

Mercie said this was because he didn't believe in a king. "You have to believe," she always explained, "in order to see." That didn't make sense to Hero. The Enchanter had said the opposite: "Seeing is believing." It was all well and good for everyone else in Great Park to talk about a king. But how was Hero to know they weren't playing a game with him? Or pretending?

At any rate, he wasn't in the mood for such games today. Mercie had said that a friend of hers was coming this morning to look at his brother. Something was wrong with Little Child. Mercie said he was too old to be unable to speak, and that all normal children were full of laughter. Something must have stunned this little one, something that had knocked the words and laughter from him.

Hero knew it was the Enchanted City. Its sour odor sat upon their hearts. He remembered the Burners igniting the bier at his mother's funeral. He saw again the stricken look in his brother's eyes. Now the younger boy could no longer laugh, and the older would not play games.

Watching his brother sit quietly on the still man's lap, Hero wondered: *Did Mercie's friend also know what to do for a boy whose scar went deeper than his skin?*

Hero thought he heard someone call, "Sighting!" But instead of the King, a peasant stepped into the cottage. He was wearing a collarless shirt and worn breeches. His hair curled beneath an old, brimmed hat, which he hung beside the door. He banged cheerfully on the doorpost. He called, "Where's my friend?"

Hero thought he'd meant Mercie, but instead the old woman pointed to Little Child sitting by the window. "Here he is," she said. "Here's your friend."

The peasant laughed. "I thought my friend would like to go with me today. We can watch the sun make the grapes fat. Or we can listen to the bees singing in the flower garden. Or we can race the ducks across Duck Pond." He produced a birch bark boat, with tiny sails and small acorn people.

The man handed the toy to the child, who took it carefully. Then suddenly, the peasant did a flip, and then walked around the room on his hands. Hero gasped in surprise and Mercie laughed.

The peasant walked to the door, his feet waving in the air. "Come on, my friend, let's go see the ducks!"

To their amazement, Hero's brother climbed down from the still man's lap. Mercie handed the child the peasant's hat, and he followed the upside-down figure out the door and down the path. Hero thought he heard the beginnings of a boy's chuckle.

Hero stayed around the cottage all that morning. In a way, he wished the peasant had asked him to go along. He chopped wood for the fireplace, careful not to get too close to the fire. He fed the pigs. He helped Mercie care

64

for Man-Who-Sat-Like-Stone. He swept the floor.

Early in the afternoon, a young man returned, carrying Hero's brother asleep in his arms. The little boy's thumb was in his mouth. There were berry stains on his cheek and chin.

"Well, we had quite a morning," said the young man after Little Child had been placed in bed. Hero and the man sat at the table, waiting as Mercie poured cold juice from a stoneware pitcher.

"Where did the peasant go?" Hero asked.

The young man smiled. "To find the King. It's Sighting Day, you know. . . . Say, have you ever heard a bee chorus? We did. It's amazing! They buzz in harmony. There was one old drone who was off tune, but the queen soon silenced him."

Mercie laughed.

"Then, we raced boats. There were fifty ducks and fifty boats and hundreds of children. The ducks won. But our boat came in second." The young man looked around, then spoke behind his hand. "Your brother and I blew hard into the sails!"

Hero didn't know whether to believe him or not.

"And, oh, yes! We watched the grapes grow." He motioned to a bowl of fruit on the table. Hero had thought they were plums, but now he saw that they were huge grapes plucked off the stem. "Uh, we watched too long—I was telling a story. Sorry, but they're still good. Try one."

Hero reached over and bit into a grape. It was luscious. He scratched his head. How had the grape grown so large?

The young man was still talking. ". . . and, you'll be glad to know, your little brother laughed. He loves to see people walk on their hands." He rubbed his arms and shoulders. "And Little Child talked. He said, 'I see da Keeng.' "

Mercie was sitting at the table with them. "Most appropriate," she said, "for Sighting Day, don't you think?" With that, she got up, walked over, and planted a kiss on the young man's head. "I knew you could help him. Thank you for your time."

Hero looked at Mercie. Who was this young man? What had happened to the peasant?

"Don't mention it," the young man was saying. "It was wonderful fun. Now, I'm going to the practice field. The children are all waiting there. You come, too, Hero. This is one of the best days there is."

And Hero soon discovered the young man was right. Sighting Day was great fun! The man organized games and competitions. There were three-legged races and pole vaulting and hide-and-seek and human pyramids and walking the log. Hero found himself drawn into the middle of all the joyful clamor. He discovered that no place was more fun than the place where the young man was.

The man taught them all to walk on their hands. The children struggled to perform the feat. Their elbows collapsed; their legs refused to stay straight up above their heads. Their feet tilted too far over. Who-o-o-o-oa! Down they fell! Everyone was laughing.

"See," said the young man to Hero. "This exercise is great for making unhappy children laugh."

The young man juggled with the Clown Juggler; they almost dropped oranges and almost bungled the throws and almost missed catching the falling objects. All the children laughed and clapped and cheered.

And everyone shared jump ropes and balls and marbles, and no one was left out of the games, and no one was chosen last.

The play ended when all the hot and sweaty children traipsed to Lake Marmo, where they plunged into the cool water and splashed and dunked the young man, who splashed and dunked each back. Hero had to admit that it had been a wonderful afternoon. Games were not so bad after all.

By the time young man walked back to Mercie's cottage with Hero, Little Child was eating his supper. "I see da Keeng!" he shouted and ran to greet his friend.

These words were the first Hero had ever heard his brother speak. The older boy's eyes suddenly felt moist, and he turned to the young man and said a choked, "Thank you."

Mercie served them the grapes that were so big they made you laugh just to look at them and some bread and cheese. Hero took a bite of the fruit and thought he had never tasted anything so good.

"I see da Keeng," said Little Child, smiling and playing peekaboo with his pudgy hands.

"Do you really think he saw the King?" said Hero.

Mercie looked at him in surprise, then slowly answered, "Yes!"

Hero's face had a frown. His happiness was fading into disappointment. "Well, why can my brother see the King when I can't?"

Mercie looked at the young man with a question in her eyes.

Quietly, he bent and tousled Hero's hair. "Your brother can see the King because he is a little child, and little children play the game best of all. The others see the King because they believe and have been given the gift of seeing. Here in the park, believing comes before seeing."

"But will I ever see the King?" asked Hero.

"Do you believe in the King?" asked the young man.

"I don't know. I think maybe, but if I could only see . . ."

"Well, someday, you just might," said the young man. He plucked another giant grape from the bowl and handed it to the boy.

That evening, after everyone in Caretaker's Cottage was quiet, the Caretaker took Hero to Outcast Village. As they walked, the soft jingling of the

66

tools in the man's pockets made a comforting sound in the dark.

Caretaker explained that on Sighting Day many outcasts were unable to play the game of hunting the King. Some were wounded. Some were blinded. Others were mending from their diseases. Instead the King came to them. He sang songs and told stories. He wove moonlight and the warm night and all good things together until the hearts of the outcasts were comforted because the King had been among them.

Unfortunately, Hero was too far away to see the King. There were too many people crowded around. The night was too full of shadows. But he heard a man's voice lifted into the sweet night air. Then all the people sang along. Soon that song ended and another began.

The boy felt strangely peaceful and thought that the ugly burn on his face might not really be so important.

Someone began to walk among the people. Hero could see a form moving closer to him, stopping and talking to each outcast. He hoped it was the King.

Hero peered into the night. It was—it was only a beggar! The man was wearing a brown cloak and hood.

"Hero?" the beggar asked. "Hero? Don't you know me?"

Hero wanted to say, "You're nothing but a beggar," but something in the man's voice stopped him.

"You must see me with your brother's eyes," the beggar said. "You must see me as he sees me."

The beggar took off his hood and cloak. Hero tried to see him with his brother's eyes, his brother, who had sighted the King. And then . . . why—why, yes, it was the peasant who had come into the cottage that morning and carried Little Child off.

"Hero!" said the peasant. "Can you do this?" He sprang onto his hands and balanced his feet in the air as he moved across the grass.

Hero hadn't spent all afternoon at the practice field for nothing. He lifted his hands above his head, then went down to the ground with his feet in the air. He walked around awkwardly until he faced the peasant. They looked at each other upside down.

The peasant now wore the face of the young man. Hero began to laugh. "Yes," he said, just before he lost his balance and he tumbled to the ground. "You're the young man—"

Suddenly it all came together. Hero understood. This was the King. This beggar. This peasant. This athletic young man. Here was the one who had made his brother laugh, and had helped him speak. This was the one who had poured joy into Hero's heart and taught him that games were fun.

The King sat on the grass beside Hero. The Sovereign was laughing. So was Caretaker. Hero could hear him jingling and chiming. "This is the King," said the old man.

"I know," said Hero. He rose to his feet. He flipped to his hands. He walked awkwardly with his feet in the air, balancing, tipping, then righting himself.

Then he faced the men. He said, "I see the King!"

And he did.

And so the boy discovered that seek-the-King is a wonderful game. Like all games it must be played with a child's heart, which believes and is always prepared to be surprised, because a King can wear many disguises.

Two Noisy Knights

There were two knights in Great Park who thought they were Rangers. The people of the Kingdom called them Sir Bumpkin and Sir Pumpkin and tried to be understanding, but knights had long ago gone out of style.

Sir Bumpkin was long and thin and farsighted. He was always tripping on roots and bushes and stones because he couldn't see the danger that was near. Sir Pumpkin was round and short and nearsighted. He was always getting stuck in tight situations, because he squinted to see the danger that was far off.

The two knights always attended Ranger councils in the Ranger Lodge. At the end of each meeting, after all reports had been made and all tales had been told, the Ranger Commander would ask for the pledge to the King. He would shout, "How goes the world?"

And all would answer back, "The world goes not well! But the Kingdom comes!" Each Ranger, to a man and woman, raised his hatchet and vowed, "To the Kingdom and the King!" Then they marched from the lodge to take up watch or to go on patrol.

The two knights would shout these same cries. They would draw their swords from their scabbards. Then they would rush from the lodge with the others—and lead their horses to a large stone. Bumpkin, grunting and groaning, would push the heavy Pumpkin into his saddle. Then Pumpkin, in turn, would pull the gangly Bumpkin into his. Often, one would drop a sword or banner.

"Yoo-hoo! Yoo-hoo!" they would shout. "You over there! Would you mind getting my sword (or banner)?"

If no one seemed to be around, they yoo-hooed all the louder. When no one appeared, one of the knights would have to climb down, and then mount all over again.

By the time both knights were seated on their steeds, the Rangers would all be gone. The lights in the lodge would be dark, but Pumpkin would shout anyway, "Onward! Onward under the banner of the King!"

But alas, they never seemed to find the service they sought, for the danger was always over when they reached the scene.

"It's the spirit that counts," Sir Bumpkin reminded Sir Pumpkin one day when they were both feeling a little low. So they made up a spirited song.

> A Ranger is a Ranger is a Ranger.
> His shout is dreadful bale.
> He keeps the park from strangers
> With his awful, mighty hail.

Wouldn't you know that on this very afternoon, they engaged the enemy. Or at least, they thought it was the enemy.

"Halt! Who goes there?" cried Sir Pumpkin. His weak eyes couldn't quite make out the man running hurriedly up the path, but he thought he could see clearly enough to know that the figure was carrying a weapon.

"Halt?" questioned the man. "Why, it's me. The Baker." The Chief Baker was hurrying from the kitchen with three loaves of hot bread fresh from the oven balanced on a baking paddle.

The two knights thought he said, "A Breaker." Breakers were the Enchanter's huntsmen. Everyone in Great Park was thankful when Rangers caught these spies, so the knights had visions of glory.

"We'll teach you a thing or two," yelled Bumpkin and reined his steed to one end of the path. Pumpkin clattered to the other end, then turned toward the Chief Baker in the middle.

Both knights fixed their visors. Both steadied their jousting poles. Both horses pawed the ground. Both breathed hot air from their nostrils.

"Charge!" screamed Pumpkin. "On we go!"

Both knights pointed toward the little baker, who was carefully carrying his three loaves on the long-handled paddle. Between the one's nearsight and the other's farsight, they completely missed their opponent and neatly knocked each other out of the saddle.

The Chief Baker was unharmed. But, his fresh loaves were trampled in the dirt.

"Now *I'll* teach *you* two a thing or two!" he yelled in anger, and thumped and thwacked the two knights on their heads with his wooden breadboard. When he left, their armor was all dents and bashes. But Bumpkin and Pumpkin knew better than to talk about this hapless adventure.

A few weeks later, on the Day of Appointments—when merits and ribbons were awarded to various Rangers—the two knights were a little late arriving at the lodge. They had been so excited as they helped each other into their armor that their suits had become entangled. By the time they were unstuck and on their way, they arrived to find the lodge dark. They peeked in anyway.

It was very quiet inside, more quiet than they had ever heard it before. Someone was sitting in the front of the lodge on the platform. It was Ranger Commander.

When the two knights entered, the Commander rose to his feet. "Sir Bumpkin and Sir Pumpkin, I have been waiting for you. A grievance has been filed against you by the Chief Baker, among others. You have been accused of masquerading as Rangers. Stand forth!"

The two knights stepped forward. *Clang! Clatter! Cre-ee-ee-ak!* Their armor rattled as they marched toward the platform. Both were wearing purple plumes in their helmets, which they had given to each other for good sportsmanship and knightlike conduct.

"Have you any scars or wounds from helping others?" the Ranger Commander asked, very quietly. Bumpkin started to mention the time Pumpkin had been rusted shut in his suit of armor and Bumpkin had pried him loose, but he thought better of it. The knights shook their heads no. Their helmets rattled.

"Have you ever fought fire in the forest?" Though the Commander was not shouting, his voice echoed in the empty hall.

They shook their heads again. Sir Pumpkin lost his footing a little, tripped over his own standard, and staggered a few paces.

"When have you protected Great Park from its enemies?"

Sir Bumpkin stuttered, "N-n-n-never, S-s-s-sir." He knew better than to mention their challenge of the Chief Baker.

But, as if he had read the knight's mind, the Ranger Commander brought up the incident himself. "You fought the Chief Baker, whom you mistook for a Breaker, but you did so to seek glory for yourselves, not to protect Great Park. You wish to be honored as Rangers. But you have not acquired the fighting skills, the equipment, the courage."

Sir Pumpkin had recovered his balance. He said, "Sir, we are very good at Ranger *shouts*. We have composed battle songs."

The two knights stood straight. They threw back their heads. Their plumes bobbed, and one fell out. They shouted, "Onward for the Cause!" They shouted, "After we go!" They gave the Ranger call, "How goes the world?"

They started to sing, "A Ranger is a Ranger is a Ranger . . ." But Ranger Commander was so quiet, and the lodge was so still, that the song just dwindled away.

Their leader's eyes were flashing. "Don't you know," he asked in a whisper. It was the loudest whisper they had ever heard, and it echoed through the hall: "know-know-know-know."

"Don't you know that the Kingdom is not noise but power?"

"Power-power-power-power." This echo surged even louder through the hall.

72

Ranger Commander planted his feet firmly apart on the platform. He raised his arms in a great sweep. "Like this!" shouted Ranger Commander. A wind began to blow. *Whoo-ooo-ooo-whoosh!* The knights held onto each other to keep from being blown away.

"And like this!" spoke Ranger Commander again. Light filled his body and shone as a bright torch through the dark building.

"And like this!"

Crack! Lightning flashed. Thunder rolled. Moments later, rain came. The wind lifted the lodge from its foundations. Round and round and round it spun, up into the sky. The two knights tumbled from wall to wall, but the man on the platform stood still, glowing in the light, his arms raised, his feet firm, and his eyes flashing stars.

Finally the wind settled the lodge on the earth. The rain stopped. The lightning was gone. The thunder ceased. All was quiet, and the hall became completely dark again.

Out of the quiet came Ranger Commander's voice. "From henceforward take no name unto yourselves that you do not deserve. You are *not* Rangers. You do not defend the Kingdom or protect the outcasts or fight the enemy. Do not mistake other people's deeds for your own. Do not mistake words for daring. You may find your own place in the Kingdom—but do not pretend to take another's!"

All was quiet again. The only sound was the Ranger Commander's footsteps as he briskly walked out of the hall. The two knights stood for a long time in the stillness. It was the first time they had ever known the power of silence.

Bumpkin and Pumpkin never again said they were Rangers—or even thought of it themselves. They never went on patrols or stood beneath the watchtower shouting the Ranger cry.

Instead they decided to live near Stonegate Entrance and conduct welcome tours for newcomers to Great Park. They gave free rides on their steeds and made small children laugh and told stories of the brave deeds of Rangers. And they were content with their own place in the Kingdom.

And so the two knights never again mistook themselves. For when one has seen and heard and known the real thing, one never again confuses noise with power.

Princess Amanda and the Dragon

Once, tall grasses grew by Lake Marmo. Each spring, damsel dragons dropped out of the sky, trampled nests in the reeds, laid clutches of eggs, and buried them in the sand. And once they had given birth, the great reptiles flapped away.

Dragons in the sky are the first sign of spring in Great Park. The children come, baskets in hand, eager for dragon egg hunts. They shed their winter stockings and wiggle their bare toes in the warm sand. They race each other, laughing and breathless, to see who will reach a clutch of dragon eggs first. They yell and hoot when they find the treasure.

"Dragon eggs!" they cry. Soon the shout—"Dragon eggs!"—echoes back and forth from both sides of the lake.

Children know they are forbidden to keep dragon eggs, because a dragonet soon hatches from the egg and it achieves full growth six months later. The baby dragon's scales harden. It begins to breathe fire. At first, there are short blasts of warm air, then later great searing torches of flame. The dragon has become cunning and cannot be trusted. So a sign on the shores of Lake Marmo reads: It Is Forbidden to Keep Dragon Eggs.

The two eggs Princess Amanda found one day many months after Hero's arrival were bronze. They glowed like amber jewels in the sunlight. Perhaps she meant to carry them to Caretaker. Perhaps she thought that they were old and shriveled inside. Perhaps she forgot. But she did not take them to Caretaker's cottage.

Instead she hid the eggs. She hid them in My Very Own Place, her den in the hollow of a mighty oak on the edge of Outpost Meadow, which was so far from Stonegate Entrance that few strangers walked to it. It was so peaceful here that Caretaker visited this area only a few times in his yearly rounds.

The spring sun reached the floor of Amanda's den and warmed her hiding place. Soon, one egg rattled when the princess picked it up to inspect it. Obviously, there was no life inside. But the other one began to crack. By midmorning a dragon hatchling pecked its way out and left the shell. The baby dragon squawked for food. Its long neck bobbed and weaved. Its feet pattered back and forth, running to keep up with its huge head. It bumped into the side of the tree. Amanda laughed.

"I must take you to Caretaker," she said aloud. "He will know what to do about surprise hatchlings."

The little beast turned its brown eye on her and a great tear dropped onto its breast. Amanda began to love the baby dragon. Though she knew it was forbidden, she kept the hatchling for a pet. *Just for a little while,* she thought. *Perhaps I can tame it.*

The princess fed the baby insects and wild roots. She kept it alive with hour-by-hour feedings. And because she nurtured the hatchling, she loved it all the more. The dragonet's bare skin soon became covered with soft scales, bronze and dazzling in the sun.

That summer was filled with dragonet games. The little beast and Amanda set up relay races with the butterflies. Lines of flittering wings and one sweaty princess and one growing dragonet raced through Outpost Meadow. Other days Amanda and the animal bounded over the meadow buttercups, seeing who could take the longest leap. Soon the dragonet won every time.

Sometimes Amanda tossed her ball as high as her arm could throw, and the dragonet would spring, almost to tree line, and grab it in his jaws.

"I have perfect aim. He has perfect catch. We must be a perfect match," she sang as they played in the sun.

By the middle of summer, the dragonet was large enough for Amanda to wedge herself between the spikes on its back. Together they leaped above the meadow, flying in and out of the limbs and leaves of the old trees that bordered the open field. The dragonet let out a joyous "Cree-ee-el!" and Amanda laughed with glee.

Up and down, they soared. Up high into the tree branches and down low into the flowering meadow. Amanda hung on for her life while the dragonet flew, flapping its wings.

Amanda soon discovered that her pet hated to be left by itself. It wailed piteously when she left it to perfect her aim on the practice field, so she began to practice less and less. The dragonet particularly hated to be left alone at night. Since the princess dared not bring it to Inmost Circle—and even feared for its life should it be discovered—she began to stay away from the Great Celebrations.

One night she crawled into her den beside the beast, and he licked her face and hands. Gratefully, it stretched beside her, panting with relief that she had stayed. She could hear distant music from Deepest Forest and missed her friends. Raising a hatchling was more demanding than she had thought. Amanda became angry at the law that kept her from sharing her pet with the others. *What harm is one small dragon?* she thought.

That same night she noticed a yellow gleam flickering in the beast's eyes as it looked at her. When it licked her face, she could feel that its breath was warm and dry.

After that, when Amanda returned from short trips to forage for their food, she would find the walls of her den scorched. The hollow was becoming more blackened. It smelled of charcoal. The dragon was always glad to see her, but she was careful not to stand directly in front of its nose and mouth.

More and more often, she had to be careful of its tail. A full-grown dragon's tail is deadly. Its powerful sweep can move boulders or knock down medium-sized trees or cripple a man. *Or kill a Princess.*

Once, when she wanted to hop on its back for a ride, the dragon leaped up without her. "Cree-ee-l! Cree-ee-l!" Its cry became defiant as it shot a flame in her direction. For the first time, it had willfully disobeyed her.

As each week passed, Amanda began to laugh less and less.

One day, after racing the dragon through the forest, she left it napping in a sunny glade and returned to the hollow tree just as Caretaker was backing out of it. His sapling hat pulled out of the hole like a cork out of a bottle.

"What is wrong with the inside of My Very Own Place?" he asked. "Amanda, you haven't been lighting fires, have you?"

"Oh, it's been that way a long time," she lied. "I don't know what caused that. Maybe Burners were here last winter."

Amanda wished Caretaker would stop wearing that ridiculous tree for a hat. How could she have ever thought it so wonderful!

Caretaker stared at the dirt in front of the den. He pushed it with his foot. "Ever see any dragons around here?" he asked quietly.

"Dragons?" answered Amanda, quickly. "Not now. The season for dragons is over."

Caretaker didn't say a word, but began to walk down Meadow Path. *You old fool,* thought Amanda. It was then that he stopped and turned and looked at her sadly.

"If you ever need me, Amanda, just call." Caretaker gazed at Amanda for several long minutes, then turned around again and went on his way.

The next day, she hid the dragon in another part of the forest. When she returned, it was Mercie who sat outside of her den. *She's the ugliest woman I've ever seen,* thought Amanda with surprise. She dreaded talking to her. *Why don't they just leave me alone?*

"Amanda!" Mercie called with a sad smile. "I saw you coming before I heard you. Whatever has happened to your laugh?"

Amanda did not know how to answer. Had she changed? Everything looked different now. Was she losing her gift of seeing? Or were things appearing now as they really were? Maybe the Great Celebration was just a bunch of foolishness.

That same night, Amanda realized that the scales of the dragon sleeping beside her were very hard. She knew that its big body was crowding My

Very Own Place, and that grown dragons were no laughing matter.

This was the last night she would allow the dragon to return from its hiding place to sleep with her in the den. The next day she took it deep into the forest and commanded it to stay. Secretly, she hoped the beast would fly away. It had become too big, and Princess Amanda was afraid. Somehow, she had to get rid of the dragon. Trouble was ahead. She could feel it.

One morning a few days later she woke early. With her eyes still closed, she enjoyed the comfort of having enough room to stretch. It was a crisp fall day. She could smell the cool, dry air. And she could smell . . . fire! Amanda leaped to her feet. Fallen leaves had been pushed in a pile beside her hollow tree door. They were burning. Amanda rushed out, stomping and scattering. Her bare feet felt singed.

Looking up, she saw that an old stump was smoldering beside Meadow Path. Underbrush was smoking on the edge of the forest. Amanda could see something large and bronze-colored moving between the trees. She dashed in to put on her shoes and rushed back out.

"Wait! Wait!" she shouted. She began running along the path. "Wait for me!" She was terrified that the dry grass would catch and begin to flame from the dragon's breath. In her mind, she could see the whole forest burning, the creatures running and—oh, how awful!—fire in Great Park! Fire because of her!

Suddenly, she knew. *Great harm could come from one small tame dragon. Small tame things grow into big wild beasts.*

Where, oh, where, was Caretaker now? Why had she not taken the hatchling to him right away? Why had she lied?

The beast finally heard her call. It stepped out of the trees into the meadow to face her. Amanda gasped. It had grown even more, and she had not noticed how much.

The huge beast sat waiting for her. Its long tail swept slowly across the ground behind it, then flicked, then swept back. The claws on one paw flexed, tearing the thatch and soil beneath it, then opened, then flexed again. A thin, wet trickle dripped out of its mouth, down its jaw. Yellow light gleamed in its eyes. The dragon had become cunning. Why had she not seen this?

Amanda drew herself to full stature. She ignored the throbbing in her feet. "Dragon," she announced in her most majestic tone, "you must go. You are too big for my den. Grown dragons are not allowed in Great Park. Your breath is too hot. Fly away!"

The dragon leered at her. It hunched, like a cat on the prowl, and moved closer and closer to her. Finally, the huge beast was near. It swept its tail, which quickly covered the distance between them. Amanda hopped over the tip. The dragon swept the long jagged tail back, faster. She hopped again. It raised its head and blew hot flame onto the grass behind her. She could hear

77

the vegetation crackling. She could feel it beginning to burn. She turned and stamped the fire out. The dragon breathed again. More fire.

Her heart filled with terror. *One small princess cannot put out all the fires this one large dragon starts!*

The dragon breathed again. The flames licked her clothes, her hair. She slapped at the fire with her hands. She rolled on the ground. She could see the great beast inching closer, flicking its tail, the yellow light growing brighter in its eyes. Amanda backed away. She knew it was useless to run. The dragon always won the races.

"Oh, help!" she cried. "Caretaker! Caretaker! I am too small for this terrible dragon. Help!"

Suddenly, she scarcely knew how, Caretaker was standing beside her. He must have come bounding the moment the flames had begun.

"Kill it! Kill it!" Amanda screamed. The great beast began to lurch. It raised itself on hind legs and roared. Flying flames filled the air.

"No, Amanda," said the old man, "I cannot kill this dragon. Only the one who loves a forbidden thing can do the slaying. You will always hate me if I do it. Only *you* can slay this dragon."

Caretaker pulled his woodsman's hatchet from the silver belt around his waist. He held it erect before him. He lifted his eyes to the sky. "In the name of the King, Amanda. For the Restoration. . . . You must slay the dragon!"

Caretaker tossed the hatchet directly overhead. It flew high, then started to tumble down, end over end. The humming began, the singing the princess had always loved. The hatchet landed at her feet; its blade stuck firmly in the ground. Amanda reached down and gripped the wood. She felt the hatchet's power as she pulled it from the soil.

By this time, Amanda had backed almost to the middle of Outpost Meadow, and Caretaker had moved out of the circle of mortal combat. Small fires were burning here and there on the grass. The princess must do this work quickly. She would only have one chance.

Suddenly, Amanda had a terrible thought. Her laughter was gone. Her seeing had disappeared. What if the gift of perfect aim had vanished as well?

The dragon was very close. She kept an eye on its tail. Though she had kept the beast alive, she knew it wanted to tear and devour her. The tail moved. Amanda leaped over it. It swept back. This time Amanda was ready. She whacked the huge tail with her hatchet. Hurrah! A long piece wiggled on the ground, oozing green dragon blood.

Perhaps there is hope, Amanda thought. *That was pretty quick aim.*

The dragon cried a terrible "Cree-ee-el! Cree-ee-el! Cree-ee-el!"—not so much from pain as from rage. It reared back on its hind legs, opened its mouth, and let out a fiery blast that caught Amanda full in the face. She could feel hot flames licking her hair, her clothes.

"Now, Amanda!" called Caretaker. "Now or never!"

She took careful aim, raised the hatchet, sighted the bare white patch on the breast of the weaving dragon, which was the beast's only vulnerable spot. "For the King!" she screamed. "For the Restoration!" Strength filled her arm. She let the hatchet fly.

At that same moment, the beast roared again. It caught Amanda's leg with the bleeding stump of its swishing tail. She went down onto the grass.

But Amanda's aim was true. Caretaker's hatchet hit its mark, and the great dragon came crashing down upon the little girl. Green ooze splashed over Outpost Meadow and covered the princess.

I am dying, she thought. *I will smother under this dragon's heavy body.*

Amanda felt Caretaker's hand touch her arm. Slowly, ever so slowly, the old man raised the edge of the great dragon hulk, just enough so that Amanda could inch her way along the ground to freedom.

Then Caretaker cradled the child in his arms in the middle of Outpost Meadow and wept. Amanda's hair and eyebrows and lashes were burned into crinkles. Her clothes were charred. Her face and feet were all blisters and boils and soot. She was covered with dragon's blood. She looked like an outcast.

But the Princess Amanda had won the battle. She had slain the dragon she loved.

So the princess discovered that when one loves a forbidden thing, one loses what one loves most. This truth is a hard won battle for each who finds it and is always gained by loss.

Fire In the Forest

And now, evil lifted its head at the noise of chaos. As smoke billowed from Great Park, dark figures began to advance out of the Enchanted City. . . .

Caretaker rushed into the cottage carrying Princess Amanda in his arms. He laid the child on a cot. Mercie gasped to see her. "What has happened?" she asked.

"Fire fighting," the old man answered and the look he gave his wife told all there was to tell: Because of Princess Amanda's disobedience, Great Park was now vulnerable to danger.

Croi-e-e-e-e-e-e-e-e! Croie! Croie! The Ranger horns blasted the warning over and over. Fire! Danger!

"Do what you can for her, but quickly!" Caretaker ordered, hurrying toward the door. "Then come to Inmost Circle. The Enchanter's men are rushing the gate. You will be needed right away."

Immediately, Mercie turned and went to the fireplace where she quickly mixed together a basin full of herb salves. "Hero," she called, "I need your help. Dip these clean rags into the bowl. Then cover the child's burns. Like so."

Mercie cut away Amanda's singed clothes and covered her with a blanket. Hero watched as the old woman patted compresses into place on all the scorched and burned skin. She took a mug and filled it from the jug of healing draught. Gently, she poured it down Amanda's throat.

Croi-e-e-e-e-e-e-e-e! the horns sounded, urgently.

"I must go," Mercie said to Hero. "Danger has breached our gates." The old woman paused as she went out the door. "If you are threatened in any way, do not be afraid. Speak the Ranger cries to give you strength: 'To the Kingdom! To the King!' "

Then she was gone.

Hero watched the wounded girl, so still on the cot. What had happened? Her blistered skin, her closed and swollen eyes, frightened him. She scarcely seemed to be breathing.

Frantic noises from outside intruded into the silence of the cottage. All the able people of Great Park were hurrying toward Inmost Circle where the Sacred Flames were being lit. Hero heard Ranger shouts, heard the warning horns sounding over and over. Then from far away, he heard the ominous, low beat of the death drums of Enchanted City. His ears picked out another sound, too: *Nay-nay-nay, nay-nay-nay, nay-nay-nay.*

It was the battle song of the Naysayers, who held the power to freeze people's minds by speaking "no" into their hearts. Hero knew that Burners, spreading fires of destruction with their glowing pokers, and Breakers, carrying cudgels to beat to death those who resisted them, would be creeping behind the marching army of Naysayers.

Hero's heart filled with despair. The boy looked at the young girl on the cot. He knew she was dying. *Amanda, Amanda,* he moaned inwardly as all the memories of the little princess came rushing upon him: Amanda sitting on a stump in the woods, with flowers between her toes; Amanda throwing the Caretaker's hatchet with perfect aim to defend him against the Faithless Ranger; Amanda laughing.

Hero knelt beside the cot, his eyes wet with tears. Then he remembered Mercie's last instructions. "To the King," he whispered, choking on the words. "To the Kingdom!" His heart was heavy, but he repeated the words over and over. Suddenly a quick power seemed to fill him, a force close to anger. He stood and shouted at the top of his lungs, "To the Kingdom! To the King!"

Did the room tilt? Or was Hero simply overcome by his emotion? Amanda suddenly stirred on the cot, and Hero was aware that he could no longer hear Naysayers chanting their cry.

The girl groaned under the blankets. Her eyelids fluttered open. "Caretaker? Fire!"

Hero knelt beside her again. "He's gone, Amanda. He and Mercie and all in Great Park are hurrying to Inmost Circle."

The girl sat up, swooned, and tried again. Hero fought to keep her from rising, but she was desperate. "Don't stop me!" she screamed. "We must go! We are all in danger!"

Frantic, Hero turned to search for the healing draught of medicine. *Where had Mercie put the jug?* But he stopped when he heard someone enter the cottage. Whirling around, Hero saw a dark figure standing in the doorway. It was bent and huddled, hidden beneath the folds of a dark robe, but Hero could see the face, chalk white, with piercing eyes and a chilling grin. The intruder held an ugly club, knobbed and brutal looking, in its hand.

It crept slowly, but surely, toward the corner where Amanda rested.

Hero wanted to throw himself in the path of this terrible form, but he was as frozen as the moment, which seemed to move on crippled feet.

The Breaker raised his cudgel above his head. Amanda moaned. Then

82

from nowhere, Hero heard a shout. The stamp of rushing feet and the whirl of a flying hatchet filled the room. Then a man in a blue cloak and the ghostly Breaker were locked in a fierce wrestling match, which sent chairs and tables crashing and ended with the Breaker being hurled out the door into the smoky afternoon.

A Ranger stood in the middle of the cottage, straightening tables and chairs. He shot a grim smile at Hero and Amanda who were filled with shock. "That's one for Great Park!" he said as he tossed the cudgel, abandoned by its owner, into the fireplace.

"How? . . ." Hero asked.

The Ranger gently and carefully wrapped Amanda in a blanket. "My orders were to come get you two," he answered. "Saw him sneaking in. The lousy creatures! Always take advantage. Now the Park's full of his kind." He hefted the girl into his arms and motioned with his head to Hero. "Grab something loose fitting that she can wear. And hurry!"

The Ranger stepped swiftly out of the cottage, but Hero hesitated, his heart beating wildly at the thought of walking through a burning Great Park. Something like an unbidden prayer, or an old song half-remembered, quietly rose within him. *To the King. . . . to the King. . . .*

In one movement the boy rushed after the Ranger into the hot and strange afternoon. A strong smell of smoke choked the air. The sky above was boiling with awful, yellow gray clouds. Something shadowy caught Hero's eye. A dark form darted behind a tree, then another followed it.

When they finally reached Inmost Circle, the Sacred Flames were blazing with power. Rangers inside the circle were shouting commands as the subjects organized into striking units, fire fighters, protectors, and flame carriers.

Hero would not walk through the flames with the Ranger who carried Amanda, and even the girl shuddered and asked to stay outside the Sacred Circle. The boy and girl stood together and watched Ranger Commander beyond the fire.

The silver insignia flashed on his shoulder and his belt buckle. Mercie, now a strong war maiden, worked beside him. She passed unlit torches to some, maps to others, buckets to others.

The King stood in the middle of it all, head and shoulders above most. His face was stern, and his eyes blazed with indignation. He, too, wore the Ranger cloak, but in his hands he held a silver scepter, which radiated fiery flames.

Suddenly, the King tossed back his head and whistled. Then the Ranger Commander and his wife, Mercie, repeated the call. In an instant, great stags—the elk and the buck—stepped out of the forest, as though they had been waiting for the command. Racks upon racks of horns reflected the light from the ring of flames.

At once, the King, the Ranger Commander, and Mercie stepped outside the Sacred Flames, and leaped to the back of one of the great elks. Many inside the circle followed, until a great band of men and women were mounted on the huge animals.

At that moment a young buck without a rider nudged Hero. "Let me help you mount, Amanda. We will go with them."

The King leaned high above the withers of the elk he was riding and signaled to the troop behind him. Hundreds of mounted stags moved out of the clearing and through Deepest Forest. First the lines moved at a walking pace, then at a trot, then at a canter, tracing their way through the deer trails of the woods. Hero could hear Amanda's low moans of pain as she clung behind him.

Soon the riders fanned out in a wide arch, the flames of their burning torches weaving in and out through trees and brush. The mounted soldiers struck a song. "To the King!" The foot crews answered back: "To the Kingdom!" Hero's heart was filled with a strange courage as the chant echoed back and forth through the forest with the pounding cadence of the animals' hooves beneath it.

A band of foot soldiers broke away when the army reached Outcast Village, so they could carry the lame and crippled to a nearby stronghold, which could be protected from the onslaught of Breakers. Hero asked one of the men to take Amanda with him. Her quick nod of agreement assured Hero that he had been right: Amanda was too weak to continue on.

But Hero knew he must help protect Great Park. He followed the mounted Rangers toward Outpost Meadow where the dry grass was blazing around a huge carcass. Smoke bellowed. Great old trees were being consumed by the licking, hungry fire.

As they approached the burning area, Hero could see that each Ranger now held his hatchet up in his free hand. A hum began, the familiar anthem of power Hero had heard so often. The line of advancing fighters divided in half, each flank taking a side of the wide, burning acres. The Rangers, still mounted, lifted their voices in harmony as if to accompany the singing hatchets.

Now the King urged his great elk forward. It cantered to the very middle of the burning place, beside the hulk of the dead beast. Hero was filled with awe at the King's courage. The King dismounted, not heeding the wild fire leaping around him. He pointed his scepter toward the great ring of men and women who surrounded him.

At that instant, a great whirlwind began to blow. The fire in each Ranger's torch leaped to the next in line. A Circle of Sacred Flames bounded from man to woman to man to woman and at last was joined, one burning link spreading around the woods. The wild fire of destruction was surrounded by the flames of the King's power, which would contain the fire

84

while the Rangers fought the enemy. The Rangers shouted in one voice, "To the King! To the Kingdom!"

In the middle of Outpost Meadow, the King lifted his scepter. The woods, which had been filled with the yelps and howls of the Enchanter's minions, fell silent. The Naysayers ceased chanting. The pounding of the death drums was stilled. It was the awesome moment before battle.

Suddenly, with a terrible crash, lightning flashed from the blackened sky and struck the tip of the silver staff. White heat blazed through the form of the King whose feet were planted wide apart. His body shimmered and glistened, yet he stood firm. He held his head back and cried aloud, "To My Father, the Emperor of All! To the One Who Always Is!"

Hero realized then that the Rangers were waiting for a command. Suddenly, it came. The voice of the Ranger Commander roared through the forest. "To arms!" A hundred throats from the flanks on either side echoed back, "To arms!" Each Ranger thrust the handle of his burning torch into the forest floor and lifted his hatchet.

"Charge!" came the cry.

"To the King!" came the answer and the Rangers, mounted on elks, leaped toward the forest.

Standing outside the ring of flames, Hero realized he was unarmed for battle. Dismounting, he yanked a gnarled root, solid and lethal, from the earth. In that moment, rough hands grabbed him, throwing him against a huge oak. His breath jammed in his lungs. He felt hard blows against his chest and his shoulders. Then he heard a cry of pain. His own voice.

Instinctively, Hero fell to the ground and rolled away from his attacker. Whoom! A cudgel landed near his head. He rolled again. A near miss!

A terrible anger rushed into Hero. Through the assault he had held onto his own club. He ruthlessly plunged it into the midsection of the form standing above him. This time, he heard the stranger's shriek of pain.

Hero scrambled to his feet, his lungs starving for air. He raised his club and crashed it against the head of the Breaker.

Hero watched as his enemy crumpled into a still form; then he bent and yanked back the hood. A white face, bushy eyebrows, and a final, teeth-baring grin appalled the boy.

"Good work—" said a voice behind him. It was a foot soldier. "Get ready. Burners."

Hero drew breath finally, in long pants. "How—do you—fight—a Burner?"

"Fight fire with fire," said the soldier, and he drew two burning brands from the Circle of Flames, tossing one to the boy. "Just do what I do."

Nay-nay-nay. The ominous battle cry grew louder.

"Don't listen to the Naysayers—" warned the foot soldier. "Here come the Burners!"

A band of dark shadows sprang out of the woods. The Burners' torches glowed with lurid light. Hero's heart despaired. He remembered Branding, long ago. His stomach and back began to throb.

"Charge!" yelled the foot soldier beside him.

Amazed, Hero watched the man rush the ominous Burners.

Nay-nay-nay, thought Hero. *What is the use of one against so many?*

"Come on, lad!"

Fatigue gripped Hero like bands of steel. Despair chained his heart. How could the King win against such evil?

Burners surrounded the lone foot soldier. One of the Burners thrust a poker at him. It caught the fighter's clothes, but he whirled free, then held his torch at arm's length and turned and turned, widening the distance between himself and his enemies.

Nay-nay-nay—

"Come on, lad! Give me a hand!"

Through the fear that froze him, Hero heard another voice. "To the Kingdom!" It was the voice of the King.

Hero grabbed his brand. He screamed, "I'll give you two hands!" then plunged through the ring of Burners, flailing and thrusting with a mighty energy.

Back to back the two subjects of the King stood. Thrust! The flames leaped from the brands in their hands and curled around a Burner. "Yi-i-i-i!!" one of the Burners yelped and fled from the circle. Hero and the foot soldier whacked their torches at the enemy, knocking the pokers of two Burners to the ground and lighting the garment of another in flames. Soon this band had turned and fled into the forest.

Hero again heard the voice of the King. "To the Emperor of All! To the One Who Always Is!" Thunder rolled. And the rains came. The raging flames, which had been contained within the Circle of Sacred Flames, wavered back and forth, sputtered up and down, and finally lay still, quenched by the driving rain.

A great wail rose out of the distance. "Retreat! Retreat!" Hooves pounded in the forest as Rangers chased the evil ones through the dark night toward the keyhole entrance to Great Park.

Finally, the Circle of Sacred Flames itself blazed up high to meet the sky, and then it, too, was extinguished. Exhausted, Hero turned back toward Outpost Meadow, just in time to see the flames burn low and to see the King lower his scepter. Mercie and the Ranger Commander stood on either side of him.

Soon dawn broke, the rain stopped, and the hum of the hatchets faded away. The gates to Great Park slammed closed. The animal herd fled into the forest. And each man and woman returned to their loved ones.

Nothing remained on the battlefield where the War of Fires had been fought, but the scorched earth smelling like damp ashes, and three weary figures in the middle of Outpost Meadow: an old woman, an old caretaker, and a young peasant.

They bent their heads together and held each other. Then the peasant whispered, "To the Restoration!" and lifted his hands to the sky.

So the raging fire in the forest was quenched by a greater Power, for there are some things that cannot be moved, that cannot be shaken, that are beyond burning.

Trial By Fire

Not long ago, two children in Great Park made a quest: a boy who sought a way to walk through the thing he dreaded most and a girl who feared she had lost the One she loved most. And together they discovered the Kingdom within and without, which all do, who have the courage to make the quest.

The War of Fire had been won, but a terrible feeling of evil permeated Great Park. Dark beings seemed to lurk in every shadow and behind every tree and bush.

"Oh, Mercie. It's all my fault," Amanda cried, after she had returned to the safety of Caretaker's Cottage. "I did it. I disobeyed. Great Park has suffered because of me. We will never be the same. Never."

Mercie rocked the blistered child in her arms and wept, too. She offered the girl the healing draught and applied a poultice. She prayed for kings-love, but Amanda did not receive any comfort. A raw wound festered deep in her soul.

Later that night, Hero hurried to the Ranger Lodge where council had been called. Caretaker, not the Ranger Commander, stood on the platform since there had not been time for becoming; but the elderly man's eyes flashed bold in the old way. Not one Ranger doubted who it was in command.

"I know you are weary," Caretaker shouted, loud enough so that those in the back of the hall could hear. "We are all weary. Battle is never in the heart of a peaceable people. We all long for peace. The War of Fire has been won. But now, *now,* our work begins. The evil ones may come again to Great Park. Protection has been breached!

"There will be no rest for protectors. More care is required *after* disasters. The Burners and Naysayers will grasp any opportunity to take advantage. Watch must be doubled. Our diligence must be threefold."

The old man stopped. Hero watched as he lowered his head. He looked worn, ancient, and a little foolish. But the boy loved him with his whole heart.

"We must take time for the Ceremony of Purity. If any lust for battle has entered your heart, if any love of the leaping flames or any shadow has lodged in your soul, it must be called out. No advantage shall be given to the enemy by the protectors! None!"

Caretaker lifted hands, which were gnarled and veined, in invitation. "Come," he called, "renew your vows to the King! There will be no Great Celebration until the danger is over."

Hero watched as the men and women bowed their heads. Silence settled down upon the hall like a great, winged bird that smothers all noise beneath its soft, down breast.

The press of quiet was awesome. Some went to their knees. Some stood with tears streaming down their cheeks. Hero thought about the Viewing Circle where he had seen a faithless Ranger revealed. The boy listened to his own soul. Flames flickered in his mind. An old wound throbbed.

Hero heard footsteps across the wood floor, coming from the far back. Then the sound of other footsteps from another place—and more and more and more.

"I am for the King and for the Restoration," said the one. The voice was low.

"I am for the King and for the Restoration," said the next. And on and on.

As the boy listened, he realized he, too, was for the King. There was no other place he desired to be, no other way he wanted to live his life. He made a deep vow: *I will find the courage to walk into the Sacred Flames. I will become a part of the Great Celebration.* But he did not follow the others to the front of the hall.

For now, the vow was enough. Still Hero knew that someday he, too, must walk to meet the King. Until then his quest would not be over.

For weeks, the Rangers kept double watch. They mended the breaches in the forest. The ring of acres devastated by the War of Fire was cleared to wait for spring when Caretaker would speak the magic of greening and blooming. Protectors hunted out the shadows that lurked, and the King's men chanted the King's name into the darkness to scare any evil ones away.

Hero volunteered to climb the watchtowers to relieve those suffering from fatigue. He worked with crews cutting out smoldering trees. He didn't know when or where his scorched heart had turned young again, but it had. After a while he joined the Rangers as they began to sing on their marches through Deepest Forest. Soon the Ranger cries returned to half-hour intervals rather than the recent quarter-hour watches.

"How goes the world?"

"The world goes not well."

"The Kingdom comes."

The call sounded out safety. The boy felt secure.

Finally, Great Park returned to what it had been. Men and women went back to fields and crafts and forests. Once again there was time to listen to the call of birds and to notice bees humming and to watch the sky stained pink each dawn. Plans began to be made for the first Great Celebration since the War of Fire. Spring had come. Children reminded each other of dragon egg hunts.

In all this time, neither Hero nor Amanda saw the King. Hero wished they had, for Amanda continued to sicken and wane. What was wrong with her, anyway? Hero wondered. Under Mercie's care her burns had healed. Miraculously she was not even scarred.

One day Hero came upon her sitting on the step of Caretaker's Cottage. From far away, he could tell that she was spitting at stones.

"Aha!" he shouted as he approached her. "Practicing your aim?"

Startled, she stood. "Leave me alone," she shouted. "Why don't you all leave me alone?" She kicked the raccoon that had curled in the sun beside her. "And stop looking at me," the girl sneered. "You're all ugly! I can't stand the look of your scarred face. Mercie's an old crone. Caretaker is creepy. I don't want to see any of you!"

With that, she stormed into Caretaker's Cottage. Hero could hear her topple a chair, stamp across the room, and then bang a door.

He remembered the Amanda he had once known, and did not at all like what she had become. Maybe slaying dragons was no business for a princess. At any rate, she seemed to be a princess no longer.

Hero stomped his foot, angrily turning to go—

"Hero!" Mercie called. She had been working in her herb garden and had heard every word. The boy turned toward her. She smiled and stepped between the mounds of fragrant rosemary and thyme. "You are wondering what is wrong with Amanda. She is trying to bear her own guilt; that is a burden too heavy for anyone to carry."

"She called me ugly," said Hero, surprised that it had hurt him so. In Enchanted City he had been used to people calling him Scarboy. "Am I *really* ugly, Mercie?"

Mercie handed him a trowel, and the two knelt under the sun and began to dig together in the rich soil. "No," said the old woman. "You are a handsome and strong lad; but Amanda—well, Amanda has loved something more than the King. Whenever that happens, seeing becomes dimmed and we see without real sight. All things seem ugly—most of all, ourselves."

Hero noticed the wonderful spikes of the chive. "What will help her? Will she ever be herself?"

Mercie pinched back the parsley. "The King can help her. When we walk through the Sacred Flames, we always become what we really are. Amanda needs to go back to him at the Great Celebration. The cure for disobedience is to obey again."

Hero thought about his own unfulfilled vow. "Is she afraid of the Sacred Flames?" he asked.

The old woman looked at him. She smiled and almost laughed. "You are afraid of the Sacred Flames. Amanda is afraid of the King. She is afraid he will banish her, because she has been faithless."

Mercie looked far away, as though she was seeing something far off. "We all have to walk through the thing we fear most in order to gain the thing we want most. What do you want the most, Hero?"

Hero knew. He remembered a young man's laugh, felt the brush of a brown beggar's cloak. He thought of a shadowy form, singing softly, moving among the outcasts. He felt his two hands holding the strong tug of the woodcutter's saw. He saw a beautiful man dancing behind the leaping wall of Sacred Flames and heard the music of the Great Celebration. He saw a King standing fearlessly in the middle of the War of Fire. Hero wanted to serve this man. He wanted to serve him with all his heart and mind and soul.

Mercie whispered as though she had been reading his thoughts, "Go to him. You will find him at the Great Celebration. Take Amanda with you. When we walk through the Sacred Flames for the sake of another, it is never so fearful."

But Amanda would not attend the Great Celebration. She became angry when he asked. If she was inside, she slammed doors. If she was outside, she threw stones.

Finally, Hero appealed to her sympathy. "Please, Amanda. I am afraid of the flames. Go with me. Help me."

"Go with Mercie," she spat back. "Or with Caretaker. There are hundreds of others who would make entrance with you."

Hero persisted. "No, I want you to go with me. For your sake, Amanda. How can you stand to be so far from the King?"

At that Amanda melted. It was true. She yearned to see the King, even if he sent her away. She wept. "Oh, Hero, he will banish me. I have always been his little princess, but look at me, I am a princess no more. . . . Still, I will go with you."

So the two went: the boy who had escaped from darkness because he loved light more than he knew and the girl who had become ordinary because she did not realize how wonderful it was to be a princess.

A light wind ruffled the leaves in Deepest Forest that night. The children could hear the music of Inmost Circle from afar. Amanda grabbed Hero's arm and put her hand to her throat. "Oh, Hero. What if he doesn't speak to me at all? What if he pretends I am not there?"

For the first time since they had met, it was the boy who drew her on, leading her by the hand. They approached the great clearing. Rangers stood in blue cloaks around the Sacred Flames, which were leaping higher and higher. Yet something was odd. No one was singing. No one was dancing.

Amanda let out a low moan. "Oh, no. They are all waiting for us."

It was true. All the subjects of the Kingdom were standing in small circles, talking to each other as they waited. And the King? The King—with hands crossed behind him, his hair glinting with gold, his robes and garments white and gold-flecked—walked back and forth, back and forth, within the Ring of Flames.

Amanda turned to go, but Hero grabbed her by the elbows. He was determined that her agony should end. They approached the Sacred Flames. The two knelt at the edge before a Ranger. From the bottom of his very being, Hero uttered his vow. "To the King! To the Restoration!"

Amanda was weeping, but she managed to repeat his words. "To the King! To the Restoration!"

Hero turned toward the flames. He could feel the heat on his face, but instead of terror, a joy rose within him. He was anxious to meet the beautiful King waiting for him on the other side. He was determined to be a part of the Kingdom. He was absolutely convinced that Amanda should know kingslove again.

The two made entrance.

One moment: a dimming. Then passage. A great shout went out from the other celebrants. It rang through the night, out through Deepest Forest, loud enough for all of Great Park to hear. Princess Amanda had come back! The boy Hero had carried her through the thing he feared the most.

The two children rushed toward the King, who was already moving toward them. Mercie, beautiful beyond imagining, and Ranger Commander came running. They all met each other. They embraced. They called each other's names.

Amanda wept as she looked up at the King. "I thought you would never want to see me again."

The King wiped her tears, but she wept all the more. All her sorrows tumbled out: "I disobeyed. I lied. I cursed Caretaker in my heart. I loved a forbidden thing. I brought fire into Great Park. Everyone has suffered because of me. Send me away. I don't deserve kingslove."

The King folded the weeping child into his arms. "Don't leave me, Amanda," he whispered. "We've all been so lonely without you."

Between sobs, the girl spoke. "I know—I can never be a—a princess again, but I still want to be your subject and obey."

"Look, Amanda," said the King, "look at what you have become."

Amanda glanced down. She was wearing a beautiful new gown. She lifted the folds of the skirt. There were pearls at the hem and a ring on her hand and she felt a light weight on her head. It was a small circle diadem.

The King faced her, took her hand, bowed low, and said, "You will always be a princess as long as I am your brother."

Amanda looked at the King's eyes. All at once, relief, warm and wonderful, flooded her. She threw back her head, and laughed! The celebrants heard it. They had been waiting for months. Princess Amanda was laughing again!

Mercie gathered Amanda in her arms, swept her up, and together they joined the dance that began the Great Celebration. The King walked over to Hero. He placed his arm around the young man's shoulders. "Come," he said. "I have a place saved for you beside me."

At the banquet table, Hero sat next to the King. He ate the Chief Baker's bread and thought nothing had ever tasted so good. He watched the two silly knights tell stories and sang the court's songs and applauded the Apprentice Juggler and laughed because he was part of this good company.

After a while, the King said, "Hero, I have a task for you. I wonder if you will have the courage to undertake it."

For the first time in a long while, Hero touched his cheek with his fingertips. He could feel the rough edge of the scar. He was surprised that it was still there, and even more surprised that it did not seem to matter anymore.

The King continued. "I need a King's man to live in Enchanted City. It is time to begin the Restoration of the Kingdom. I need someone with a hero's heart, someone who knows the ways of the Enchanter. Will you come?"

Hero choked on a morsel of bread he had been chewing. He stammered. "But I—but I just—"

The King laughed. "I know, you just made entrance. But I will not be leaving for a while. Take some time to learn the ways of the Kingdom. Enjoy the Great Celebration. Learn from Mercie. Walk with the Ranger Commander. When you are ready, I will call you."

Hero looked into the King's eyes. *Go back to the Enchanter and his Burners? How strange it is that I would do anything for this man! . . . But were there King's men in Enchanted City?* Hero remembered the taxi driver who had shouted "To the King!" so long ago. *Yes, maybe there were.*

The King knew Hero's thoughts. "It will be worth all the danger, Hero. I have work for you to do." He stood and turned to leave the table.

Suddenly, Hero had a terrible thought. "But, sir, how will I find you in Enchanted City? Will you be in disguise?"

The King laughed again. He reached across the table and firmly clasped the hand of the new celebrant. "That's right. You were never very good at sighting." Then he leaned over and whispered, "It won't be hard for you to find me. I will have a scar just like yours."

So the princess found kingslove. And the boy became the King's man, and discovered that one goes into the Inmost Circle in order to come out again. Entrance is only the beginning of the quest.